» Contents

I0423164

THE LITTLE BOOK OF

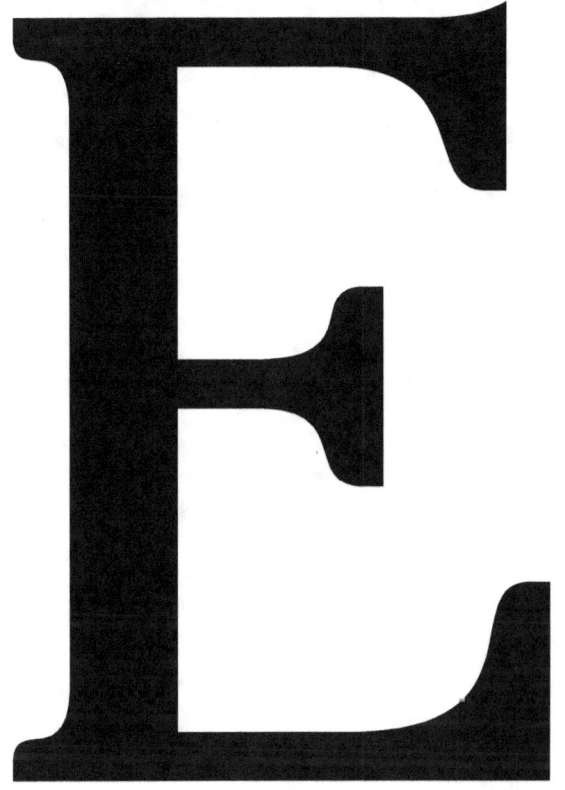

THOUGHTS ON FIXING AMERICA'S PROBLEMS

BY SEAN J. MCDERMOTT

ISBN: 1467918849
ISBN 13: 9781467918848

This book is not meant to be a heavily footnoted or referenced scholarly tome on the various factors that dominate and influence life on this planet and are ignored by a large majority of voters and leaders. It is one man's simple take on what used to pass for common and accepted knowledge in America.

I am hoping this book bothers a lot of people who cannot be bothered with facts or exercising their minds through critical thinking. I am hoping it gets enough voters and leaders to begin to at least think before voting and think before acting. We all need to be smarter about the choices we make, not just in voting but in everyday life and that takes being informed. Thinking and intelligence can longer be thought of as elitist qualities unsuited for the great unwashed masses. We can no longer live under a rock and expect things to get better and enjoy the blissful ignorance and baseless platitudes of politicians and leaders with agendas; we need to think now, think hard and think fast.

ENVIRONMENT. ECONOMY. ENERGY. EDUCATION. These are the tools used in an effective, long lasting nation state. They are the framework for critical thinking. You cannot have a healthy Economy without a healthy Environment. You need Energy to run that Economy. You need an Educated work force to make it all work smoothly and to maximum benefit for the Common Good.

Lately, Americans, politicians and other leaders in our nation have lost sight of what makes America run. It is not the first time. It happened in the nineteenth century and again in the 1920s and 1930s. As in the past, we have been distracted sometimes through ignorance, sometimes on purpose by various social issues, greed and other vice away from the four pillars that makeup and support an effective nation; a healthy Environment, a robust Economy, reliable Energy and outstanding Education. Only be recommitting ourselves to these four pillars of a just and stable society may we return to the government John Adams envisioned; one of laws, not of men, a country where no man, corporation or association of men have any other title to obtain advantages or exclusive privileges distinct from those of the community, than what arises from services rendered to the public.

John Adams, our second president, was a great thinker. He thought a lot about government and wrote just as fast as he thought about it. One of his classic tomes was a three volume set called a *Defense of the Constitutions of Government of the United States of America.* In this work and in his other writings, Adams formulated the constitutional American republic and with the other founding fathers implemented it. It was he who made the case for dividing the powers of our government into three branches; the executive, legislative and judicial. This three branch structure was the framework of our republican form of government, guided by our constitution. A republic governs its citizens through informed consent via representation. Adams felt that this type of government would balance individual ambitions with the desires of various socio-economic classes, all for the common good.

It is fair to say that as the twentieth century turned into the twenty first, our government ceased to function exactly the way Adams originally envisioned. Passions and intransigence rule the day. Special interests and extreme political, rather than informed and pragmatic thoughts and actions paralyze all three branches of our government. It is time to revisit our past, what our government was meant to be and reintroduce some basic concepts that have guided American thought and democracy for centuries.

What this small volume hopes to do is help all readers understand the concepts and facts behind the Environment, the Economy, Energy and the Education and then use this basic framework to think reasonably, clearly and pragmatically about the core issues facing our nation. Brush aside political notions and affiliations, use common sense, a simple visual mnemonic (the capital letter 'E') and then the actions that need to be taken become very clear. To everyone. Using this methodology we can then take on the most pressing problems facing our nation as individuals acting alone and in concert with others. We can adjust course and maintain a well grounded America for us and the generations that will follow us. This is a just and noble cause not for America alone but really for any nation on earth. We do not want to be remembered by future generations of Americans as the last citizens of ancient Rome are remembered by us; a fractured, distracted population blithely ignorant of their own impending downfall. So with this in mind, I believe we can move forward and add value to our nation using simple tools, rules and reason. The ideas presented here may not be politically popular or even attractive to certain willfully ignorant individuals but they do represent a reality in which we live and can live in better. So approach the material with a clear mind, good intentions and a willingness to learn.

....

We first start with a simple visual; picture in your mind the capital letter 'E'. Everyone knows and is familiar with its shape; it will be our memory tool. The positions of each of the four concepts are also important in relation to where they stand to construct our letter 'E'.

The main vertical portion of 'E' is our superstructure, the critical trunk upon which everything else attaches to and depends on. This vertical support is the Environment.

Think about it. The Environment is what we operate in everyday; we breathe air, we conduct commerce, we farm, we extract minerals and Energy…all from one very small and vulnerable planet circling the sun. No Earth, no Environment, no Economy. Period. Makes sense. This is our first undisputable fact. If some folk believe this is disputable then let them live on the Moon.

The first concept that attaches to the Environment trunk of the 'E' is the bottom leg; horizontal and flat and rooted securely in the ground. This is Energy. The Energy we use and consume in our everyday lives ultimately comes from the sun and is locked up in various ways here on Earth; mostly in the form of fuels like coal, wood or oil, but also in the kinetic energy of the wind and tides.

Some Energy also comes from the left over heat of formation of the Earth; water running down hill on tectonically shifted and uplifted mountains for example or geothermal Energy that takes advantage of the temperature difference between the surface and the rocks deep below our feet. An Economy needs Energy to run whether it is from burning wood, people or animal power or photovoltaic cells. No Energy, No Economy. Again indisputable and anyone who thinks otherwise should set up an Economy in a very dark closed, room and then try not to move. This is our second indisputable fact.

Our next horizontal beam in the letter 'E' is the Economy. It is the middle beam and also attaches to the Environment. Since we have an Environment and Energy we can go ahead and set up an Economy no matter how simple and basic it may first appear to be. It can start with just a person digging clay, forming a pot and trading it with another person who has extra food from a hunt. That is all it takes to generate a single commercial transaction. Hundreds of thousands of these types of transactions between people and places for goods and services create an Economy. An Economy can get big very fast.

Our last concept on 'E' is the top one, but by no means does this imply it is the least significant; it is Education. As our Economy starts to grow and we need more Energy beyond animal power or water power and the resources of our immediate Environment become scarce or more difficult to extract, we need to get clever fast about how to manage it all and make it run. Otherwise, we deplete our environmental resources to nothing, waste Energy and hollow out the Economy built on those resources thereby collapsing the society and culture created around that Economy. Hence Education.

It is worth noting that nothing in this critical thinking framework is new to human beings. Native Americans always had a respect for the Environment first and worked within their means to create a vibrant long lasting culture. Europeans understood the need to acquire resources and produce Energy to develop complex economies even five hundred years ago. They perhaps didn't understand it in a formal way until Adam Smith came along. Half the world, at least to 15th and 16th century Europeans remained undiscovered and unexploited. So they set sail looking for gold, spices, timber and anything else that they needed.

....

So now we have our visual; the letter 'E'. Environment is the vertical trunk. Energy is the well rooted base, the Economy is the middle beam and Education is the top beam. Now that we have the basic framework in place to guide our thinking about the world around us we need to outline four principles that will drive our four 'E' thought process. You may even want to think of the four principles as the bolts, rivets or welds that hold each of the four beams of the letter 'E' critical thinking framework together:

1. Every human decision or action has an impact on the Environment, either the Natural Environment or the Social Environment and many times on both. This is simple Cause and Effect. The impact may be direct or indirect, immediate or delayed, but human decisions on any scale always have an impact on the Environment.
2. Every human being on the planet, regardless of where they are born and irrespective of their socio-economic class has something to contribute to humanity. They have Self Worth. The contribution's effects can be large or small, permanent or fleeting, superficial or infil-trating. A person may contribute at the micro level of immediate family or at the macro level of the world. Sometimes that contribution may be felt at multiple levels of human interaction. In other words, every person has influence on the human condition, no matter how small or insignificant that influence may appear.
3. The Common Good, as outlined by John Adams and implemented by all our founding fathers to govern our nation is usually the central, engaging principle in our

analysis of an issue or problem that is presented to us for examination. In other words always ask at the beginning, middle and end of your critical thinking; is this solution the best one for the Common Good?

4. Everything on this planet called Earth is Interrelated and has influence on every other thing. The interrelation may not be direct, it could be very indirect but all entities on this small planet are connected to each other in some way. In other words, no system or process operates in isolation; no man is an island, no activity self contained.

....

The first two principles are basic and indisputable in their description of human nature. When we first begin to address any issue or problem, we start with the Environment, keeping in mind the impact of human decisions and the contribution of individuals to the overall human condition.

The third principle was one that was arrived at through quite a bit of thinking, deliberation and dedication on the part of Adams, Jefferson, Franklin, Madison and others in order to create the best workable system of government the world has ever seen. The results of forming a government based on ideas and not on men have so far been encouraging, but we need to refocus on what we have forgotten about the guiding principles as set forth by the founders of the republic. The concept of the Common Good is central to our understanding of how our government was intended to function.

To give a very basic idea of what the Common Good means mathematically, refer to the following graph.

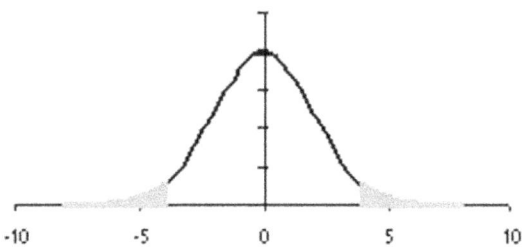

This is a graph that should be familiar to anyone with basic math skills; it is a bell curve. The curve describes the sample of a population of items or people around a mean or average; the high middle part of the curve. In this case the mean is zero as seen on the 'X' axis. The big clear middle area of the graph, which represents a standard deviation from the mean on either side of zero, is the Common Good. In other words, this is where we need to concentrate our efforts when making laws or decisions about scarce resources, Energy, Economics or about the Education of our children. The little gray tails on the left and right of the graph are outliers; things or events that don't happen so often. Not that these incidences or people should be ignored, but they should not dominate or take over the discussion or analysis that we do with respect to our laws, the direction of our nation and the future needs of our children and grandchildren.

The fourth principle is something that may not be obvious or in many cases is ignored by many people at all Social Environment levels. The interrelation of everything on earth is ignored principally because it is inconvenient to many arguments about how and why to use or conserve scarce resources on this planet. Poor decisions with far reaching and sometimes very subtle impact are made out of ignorance, convenience, laziness or expediency; what appear to be wee problems caused by poor decisions are swept under the rug. Ignore the consequences at your own risk; and maybe someone else's.

....

As we learn about the Environment, Energy, the Economy and Education we will examine the following three issues; (1) a new method of Energy extraction called hydraulic fracturing or "fracking" that uses horizontal drilling, chemicals (what are those 'chemicals' anyway?) and pressurized water to extract natural gas from deep stratified rock deposits, (2) an old form of Energy production, nuclear power and (3) a proposal for an unrestrained "no strings attached" 10% tax cut on all corporate profits regardless of business type or the size of the business.

There is a purpose for presenting these three issues in this order. The environmental impacts of hydraulic fracturing are concrete and can be felt right away during the initial process of natural gas extraction. In our examination of nuclear power, environmental issues are less tangible up front and are not so direct, but are very real at the end of the nuclear Energy conversion process. Both fracking and nuclear power are Energy processes that offer good leads to the discussion on Energy after our study of the Environment. Lastly, the Environment and Energy issues are very abstract when we begin our review of an Economic issue; an unrestrained 10% corporate tax cut.

This order of examination from fracking, to nuclear power to a tax cut follows the manner in which children and adults learn and acquire new knowledge about a subject or task the world over. Humans begin learning early in infancy. To acquire and retain knowledge, we start from concrete tangible example; then, after internalizing the new experiences the learner moves on to more abstract thought about the problem, issue or task. At the end of the learning experience, the successful student then has the ability to extrapolate what has been learned in a particular situation and apply that acquired knowledge or skill to other seemingly different or more complex situations. This model of learning is the manner and basic building block of Education and has been since the beginning of human civilization. In the Education discussion, we will cover learning tools and learning environments and how to best educate all of our children so that they may all realize their maximum potential and self worth. So, with eager eyes and open minds let us proceed.

```
E  EDUCATION
N
V
I
R          THE ENVIRONMENT is the
O  ECONOMY  circumstances under which
N          humans always operate; it holds
M          the resources we need in order to
E          create economies. Energy derived
N          from the Environment drives an
T  ENERGY  Economy. The Environment is the
```

air we breathe, the land we live on and the social space in which we conduct our daily lives. In tackling any problem, issue or task, start your thinking with the Environment first, especially the Natural Environment; it was here long before modern humans; it is still here and will be here long after humans are gone. It may change form over long periods of time but it is our constant, our tree trunk, so we begin here.

You cannot have a healthy Economy without a healthy Environment. What does this mean exactly? The Environment is the vertical trunk of our letter 'E.' It is the superstructure upon which everything else depends; the Economy, Energy and Education. A dead Environment, with depleted resources means no Energy to run an Economy.

Immediately folks think of only one Environment, the Natural Environment in which we live, breathe and eat.

They think of water and the air and trees. But there are two basic Environments that we operate in and that can be further subdivided. The Natural Environment and the Social Environment. The two Environments are interrelated; humans will interact regardless of whether they are standing on a street corner, walking through the woods, hunting on a polar ice cap or spinning around the world in a space station. All the other environments one can think of necessarily depend on the Natural and Social Environments.

To demonstrate; an Economy is a dependent process. It takes the Natural Environment to provide Energy and scarce raw materials to create goods and services and a Social Environment consisting of at least two people interacting with each other to transact commerce based on those goods and services. Now do you understand why the Environment is first on our list? It should be clear. An Economy does not stand alone. It is derived process that depends on properly functioning Environments and Energy. Another indisputable fact.

So what does this mean? The health and viability of the Environment is the single most important thing to human activity. It must be managed with care. In order to do that let us first understand some additional details about our Environment and its two major divisions.

NATURAL ENVIRONMENT

The Natural Environment consists of as many divisions as one cares to conjure up but that is not the purpose of this essay and that would be counter productive in reaching our modest goal of improving our critical thinking. So to keep things simple let us limit the subdivisions of the Natural Environment to known and unknown.

The unknown Natural Environment consists of space beyond Earth's orbit, the deepest parts of the seas and the interior of the Earth below the crust. To access these places one has to expend very large amounts of Energy. The remoteness of these regions makes the extraction and use of resources and raw materials from them too expensive to consider for everyday use by the population of the earth. In other words, the successful exploitation of resources contained in the unknown Natural Environment is pure fantasy given current levels of technology, distance and the enormous expense that would be incurred in acquiring those resources.

The known Natural Environment consists of all those resources that are naturally occurring everyday around us and are accessible with current levels of technology. These resources include iron, trees, animals, water, air, sunlight, oil and natural gas and so on that can be successfully extracted and exploited by humans for our use. Resources like natural gas and oil that are found in the ground are located in the Earth's crust, the skin of the Earth that extends just a few miles down from the surface before we hit the mantle.

It is worth noting and remembering that air, water, and other natural resources do not care about arbitrary man made boundaries. Iron ore veins and coal seams underground cross state and county lines. Water pollution upstream in one municipality does not suddenly cease at the town border. Clean fresh water, which everyone on the planet relies on to live a healthy, disease free, life is a scarce resource. Most of the water on Earth is saline and not potable. The lack of clean, fresh water is quickly becoming a limiting factor in the growth of the human population.

Pollution, like water pollution does not cease to become the polluting source's problem once it crosses a property line. There are many institutions with highly paid lobbyists or greatly outsized local influence that would have everyone believe responsibility for pollution stops at man made borders but this is not and never will be the case. Pollution is everyone's problem, across all borders in every strata of society. Its effects can be immediate and not so immediate. The invisible, not so immediate or long reaching effects of any type of pollution are scary and the most prone to demagoguery, catharsis and inaction on the part of humans. This is a fact.

Economists call pollution an 'externality,' a sometimes unexpected byproduct of human activity. An externality can be good or bad. Pollution is a bad externality. Often adverse economic externalities, especially those whose effects are not so immediate or obvious are left unchecked, ignored and passed on to someone else with less power and money to deal with because they are messy and hurt profits. But we cannot ignore pollution effects or adverse externalities in general now or in the future.

A term that comes up quite often when trying to quantify the environmental impact of a human decision or activity is 'Carbon Footprint.' What does this mean exactly? Carbon is an element locked up in living things and non-living things all over the Earth. It is what life on Earth is based on. Most carbon is locked up in plants, seashells, various rocks on and beneath the Earth's surface and under the ocean. Oil, coal and natural gas (chemical designation for natural gas: CH_4, the 'C' stands for carbon, the 'H' hydrogen) are carbon based fuels. So is wood. There is a cycle called the carbon cycle that moves carbon around and between the organic or living environment and the inorganic or physical environment. It occurs because of respiration, photosynthesis, consumption of food, the burning of wood and decomposition (think rotting plant and animal matter). Given this basic definition, carbon footprint is a measure of all the carbon associated with a given process like living, driving a car or burning fossil fuels for electricity and gages the impact of that process on the Natural Environment.

Another term that comes up often is 'fossil fuels.' A fossil fuel is created through the application of heat, pressure and time to dead and decayed plant and animal matter found in layers deep below the surface of the earth. All this old plant and animal matter dates from the time of the dinosaurs. A fossil fuel is basically carbon in some form that is found and extracted as either a gas (natural gas), a liquid (oil) or a solid (coal) that can be burned with oxygen in a process called combustion to release heat. That heat can be used for work; for example a mechanical turbine spins from steam heated by the combustion of coal to make electricity that powers your toaster so you can make breakfast. Some of the heat is wasted. All the carbon does during combustion is change chemical composition and form and then it re-enters the Natural Environment through the carbon cycle.

SOCIAL ENVIRONMENTS

The other big Environment is the Social Environment. It is the sphere of social interaction that all humans interact in everyday. I would like to break this Environment down to a few simpler social ones; the Family Environment, the Community Environment, the Regional Environment and the World Environment. These divisions will come in handy when trying to break down problems and issues into manageable components.

The Family Environment consists of one's immediate family and others that may share a home together. This is not hard and fast and the definition can flex a bit without damaging any analysis one may do. Some may wish to include extended family not living in proximity as part of the Family Environment and this is fine. Education of our children occurs at this social level. Language, behavior, social norms, problem solving, creativity and character are all hopefully being taught by parents or other responsible adults to children at this level.

The Community Environment basically involves everyone in your town or hamlet; the people that are under the direct influence of councilmen, freeholders or selectmen. It is the people you see at the local diner or in church or at the supermarket on a regular basis. Work is a component of this Environment; good and services are produced by people and machines for consumption at all levels of the Social Environment. The office or factory filled with people of various races, religious faiths, abilities and family situations is a Community Environment.

Education is a major component of this Social Environment. Teaching and instruction are more formalized at this level; most children go off to another building for the day to learn with other children, others are home schooled. Partnerships between children, teachers, parents and business are made and function at this social level to guide Education.

The Regional Environment does not have fixed geographical borders, on purpose. It may be all the people living in and influenced by a particular watershed. The watershed may cross man made, arbitrary municipal or state boundaries. But there is a common, underlying Natural Environment that ties the people together in this Social Environment. The Regional Environment overlaps with and includes states with human drawn borders. Standards for all sorts of things are set at this level; environmental, education, monetary and financial rules and regulations can originate with towns, counties or states located in a region.

The World Environment is the biggest Social Environment and encompasses all the humans living on the planet. The connection of the individual to the world can seem distant and is often under appreciated. The world does not intrude much on our daily lives. Because of this disconnect, we don't often think of ourselves in a world context. Too often real or perceived differences between people at the world level can lead to dangerous and sometimes disastrous results with far reaching consequences. The actions of a single individual or a small group of people in one corner of the globe can have unintentional consequences, good or bad, at very great distances. Cause and effect is a principle that works at the world level even if the action is at a great distance in time, in space or in both. Think of a manufacturer of solar energy equipment in the United States. Their biggest customer is in Germany. The German government shuts off a subsidy for the solar energy equipment. The customer sends an email to the factory stating they are no longer going to order the equipment. The factory in the United States has to shut down and hundreds of people are out of work, yet the action taken was by a foreign government thousands of miles away that caused the loss of domestic jobs.

Our solar energy equipment example also demonstrates how business and commerce occur across all Social Environments, through every level of human interaction. Likewise technology is a tool that is used in all the Social Environments and can facilitate communication between those environments. It is important to note that both business and technology are not universally good or universally evil. Humans need and create both for better and worse. Keep in mind that we are always working towards the Common Good, the grand middle of the statistical bell curve, therefore it is very important to see business and technology as neutral without any sort of built in bias as we train our analysis on specific issues and problems.

TECHNOLOGY

Technology is not an environment unto itself. Technology is a tool. Like a hammer or a nail gun. Technology can be used to assist teaching. Think pens and pencils, paper, laptop computers, overhead projectors and smart boards. Technology can be used to extract raw materials from the Natural Environment. Think backhoes, shovels and drills. Technology makes commerce move faster and can transport goods and services to where there is an economic demand. It is also a medium through which Social Environments can communicate and are created by the people using the medium. The first modern humans recorded information with writing or pictures on cave walls, clay tablets, pottery and clothing. Then we wrote on paper with ink and bound the loose pages into books. Then the telegraph and the telephone allowed distant parties to communicate instantly. Finally computers were invented to store and process our growing cache of sophisticated information. Then there was the internet.

The internet has thus far, at least since the invention of the written word and the telephone, proven to be a great and profound medium for humans across all Social Environments to interact in and share information. That is really magic; it has given individuals and people in Family Communities on one side of the world the opportunity to connect to any other individual or family worldwide at any time instantly, provided they both have access to the technology.

Such a powerful tool of communication can be scary. In fact, one can get sobbed (cyber-mobbed) with an overload of contacts, conflicting information and social connections. Know what you are looking for and reach out, but use caution and discretion with contacts and searches in your acquisition of knowledge. Used wisely, the internet can point the direction to and provide objective information to those who seek it and know how to filter opinion and facts properly. It comes down to knowing and trusting the references and sources and then checking the information from one source against another source. Rigor is required if we are going to use this powerful tool to better the human condition.

SCARCITY OF RESOURCES

Everything humans can exploit in the Natural Environment, whether it is food, fresh water or Energy is finite in supply. It may not seem like it in many cases but think about the world as just a little marble orbiting around the enormous sun; nothing is making the marble bigger, it is and will always be basically the same size and shape. No new mass or extra Energy beyond what the sun provides is going to be added to the Earth unless a really big asteroid crashes into the surface and then we are all in trouble.

The scarcity of natural resources is an indisputable fact. Think about fresh water for a moment. It may appear at first that there is an abundant supply of fresh water in lakes, rivers and streams and in the aquifers below the ground. Indeed in some communities and regions in the world this may be the case. But how about Sub-Saharan Africa? Somalia? India? Texas? There is even a shortage of fresh water on the small island nations of the Pacific. When we think of these terrible situations and the scarcity of a basic resource needed for everyday living then the lack of fresh water for millions of people becomes rather alarming.

To further use this example and highlight the Principle of Interrelatedness think about the Social Environments most Americans operate in; the Family and the Community Social Environments. Droughts and shortages are awful situations that happen to other people in the greater World Environment; we read about them in the news. The person in suburban New York may not think at all about a fresh water shortage. The problem is that most people do not travel beyond their comfort zone. Foreign travel is a great, mind changing exercise; more people should do it. Speaking of New York and the people living in New York City in particular, they may not have to travel very far to see how their fresh water supply from upstate in the greater Catskills region may be affected by hydraulic fracturing for natural gas in that very same region. Competing resources and interests need to be managed to maximum benefit for the Common Good and this is best done through understanding the cause and effect of human decisions and actions on the Environment, being conscious of the interrelation between different systems and processes and through conservation.

HOW TO MANAGE RESOURCES: CONSERVATION

A resource is best used when it is managed properly. Conservation is resource management. But the word conservation has taken on a different meaning in the late twentieth century. In the modern sense conservation is equivalent to hoarding resources. Conservationists would like to wall off and isolate natural resources so that no one can use them, ever. But this is not the historical meaning and not the modern one either except for the fact that many would have you believe that conservation means locking up resources and protecting them from ever being used.

Teddy Roosevelt was a conservationist. He was also a hunter and a ranchman. He understood that resources were finite and scarce and needed management in order to effectively serve the needs of our nation and humanity over the long term. He did not favor wasteful exploitation of our natural resources but a prudent use of them. That is what conservation meant to Teddy Roosevelt and others of his time; resource management.

Today in the State of Maine the art and science of conservation goes on all the time every year. Maine has a self regulating fishing fleet. The people of the fleet fish for different stocks; lobster, ground fish, dragging for scallops and so forth in different zones or sectors of Maine's waters. They get together periodically to introduce, modify, scrap and shape formulas and rules for maintaining the stocks. Lobsters of a certain size may only be caught. Dates are established for the lobster season and for who can fish where. The number of fishing licenses granted for certain fish have been limited.

Recently a quota system or 'sector management' system for various species of ground fish like flounder has been implemented. This has been done with input from local families and fishing communities, the State of Maine and regionally across the Gulf of Maine with the State of Massachusetts. Local fishermen in the various sectors can form co-ops to share the annual catch limits. The old system had a limit on days at sea. This new system allows for unlimited days at sea. In year two of the implementation of this new system, old depleted stocks are now flourishing and the fishermen are making money. The quota system has created a situation where the catch is less but the quality is higher. A new cap proposal on large haulers would spread value over the entire Gulf of Maine coast instead of it being concentrated in a few big ports. This new quota system is supported and implemented by the local fishermen in their local and regional communities. The benefits have accrued to families and to the Community Social Environments they reside in. The system is self guided through informal and formal partnerships. With input from all Social Environments and the government. The fishermen wisely exploit the bounties of their regional Natural Environment though effective conservation management. This is how conservation can and should work with all of our finite natural resources.

....

A final point to make about the Environment in general is that many of us think that those who care deeply about the Environment are flaky, tree hugging intellectuals. This is a broad generalization and is not the case for the majority of people who put Environment first in their thinking. Conservationists and others who study our environments are people who want to actively manage our resources to meet our current and future needs rather than blindly exploit them. They have the best interests of our

Environment and our daily lives at heart; not only for us living in the present but for all future generations.

ISSUE 1: HYDRAULIC FRACTURING (FRACKING)

This is a new method of extracting natural gas from the earth for use as a fuel. It uses new technologies to get at an earth based Natural Environment resource that was previously unattainable. The basic process involves vertical and then horizontal drilling deep under the ground to pockets of gas trapped in stratified and compress layers of rock. Then water, chemicals and small particles are forced into the well under pressure to open up fissures in the rock and as a result the natural gas (methane mostly) bubbles up to the surface through the drilled hole where it can be recovered, refined and used as a fuel. Burning natural gas to produce electricity is very efficient compared to coal; in fact natural gas has a lower carbon footprint when compared to coal fired power plants and thus releases less pollution in the form of particulates and greenhouse gases into the Natural Environment during the Energy conversion process.

Fresh water and natural gas are both found in the same shale under the ground in the greater Catskill Mountain Region of upstate New York and in other places around the country; Pennsylvania, Texas and Louisiana. Fresh water is scarce, so is natural gas. The gas is usually found below the depth of the fresh water aquifer. Finding natural gas together with fresh water below the surface of the earth is not uncommon; in fact it is usually the case.

During fracking operations, the gas is supposed to bubble up through man made fissures in the rocks and then through the drilled hole to the surface, not disturbing or mixing with the water in the rocks above where the gas was; at least that is the way it is supposed to work. We are told this method of gas extraction is safe and proven, but have you ever tried to control the direction and flow of bubbles in a glass of water or a champagne glass? Kind of hard to do; in fact nearly impossible. Like herding cats. So what do you think is the possibility of fracked natural gas mixing with the fresh water above it? Pretty high since we cannot control the way the rocks will fracture and where the bubbles of gas may travel. The Principles of Interrelation and Cause and Effect are at work between these two finite natural resources.

Thinking regionally, the average person in New York City may not realize that most of the fresh water they drink and use for cooking comes from two places; the Croton Watershed to the north and east of the Hudson River and the Delaware Watershed to the west and north of the Hudson River. It is the greater Catskill Mountain region and the Delaware Watershed we need to look closely at. The Delaware Watershed region is the very same area that fracking for natural gas is being proposed. Two natural and scarce resources; one is necessary for human existence and the other necessary to maintain our quality of life. Fresh water and natural gas are competing against each other.

Thinking socially in terms of health, safety and quality of life, could the fracking operations contaminate the watershed that supplies thousands of gallons of fresh water to millions of people in the New York City Community Environment everyday? The possibility is high. Where would New York City get fresh water if suddenly methane gas or other contaminants get into the supply? It is interesting to note that natural gas extraction companies are currently exempt from many work safety rules and provisions in the Clean Water Act.

What about the gains in quality of life from promised fracking jobs or land leases to the people in the Catskill Community Environment? Obviously the Principle of Interrelation is at work between the people of the greater Catskills region and the residents of New York City. It is also apparent that the Common Good principle is at work here too.

With respect to the Common Good, note the needs of the many; reliable, fresh water for millions of people in New York City outweigh the desires of the few; quality of life improvement based on promised jobs or lease contract money for a smaller population of rural inhabitants in the greater Catskill community. What if the health, safety and quality of life of the Catskill folks is also affected by bad water; if their personal family or community wells are contaminated by fracking operations nearby? What if crops go bad because of a drop in the water table or timber is lost? Catskill folks are in the first and direct line of fire if drinking water is contaminated by natural gas fracking operations. So what good is the lease money if you cannot drink the water or live in your house? Fracking does not look like a good idea from the Social or Natural Environment perspectives. The possible social gains in the Catskills do not balance out the health and safety of the inhabitants of New York City if something goes wrong with the water supply and it becomes unreliable and/or dangerous. In other words there is no Equilibrium between the two Social Environment groups; one may gain at the expense of the other and there is the possibility both groups may suffer negative consequences if something goes wrong; more on Equilibrium in the chapter on Energy.

In order to better understand the impact of natural gas fracking from the Social (health, safety and quality of life) and Natural Environment (the mixing of two scarce resources) perspectives we should reach out across social groups to gather more information. The internet and other communication mediums can help us in our quest. So can just plain talking to our friends and neighbors first. What are the experiences of small towns in Pennsylvania? Do some families or communities have methane in their drinking water? The answer is yes. Have there been accidents or spills on the surface involving those still mysterious chemicals they use to open the rock fissures in Louisiana? The answer is yes. A word on those chemicals; there are a few hundred on the approved list for hydraulic fracturing and at least two are carcinogens; benzene and formaldehyde.

Let us not forget the other social groups in the equation; the greater Regional Social Environment that includes the nation and the finally the world community. Both of these large groups could stand to benefit from fracked natural gas; the nation could get a degree of energy independence and we could export the extra gas to the world for some profit, but that will take pipelines, terminals and ships. Infrastructure improvements cost something.

But so far, at the beginning of our Environment analysis, hydraulic fracturing appears to pose some immediate and far reaching health, safety and quality of life risks. We have yet to develop the technology or the operating procedures to expertly handle any ongoing risks associated with fracking. In short, it is hard to tell bubbles of gas where to go.

But, those horrible events may happen in only a statistically small amount on instances. Think about coal for a minute. What has been the environmental cost of using coal for Energy? Thousands have died of black lung, mine collapses, and tainted water. Coal fires and strip mining have left thousands of acres of land unfit for agriculture or habitation. How do these costs stack up against the risks to health, safety and quality of life posed by hydraulic fracturing? Maybe the short and long range risks from fracking are not as costly to the Natural and Social Environments as coal mining has been over the years.

Another point to keep in mind; we have limited our discussion of the environmental repercussions of hydraulic fracturing to the New York City region and the greater Catskills Region. While it does appear that fracking in the greater Catskills Region has potentially too high an environmental impact on the millions of people in the New York City Regional Community, this is not to say that there are other less environmentally sensitive regions across the nation that have gas deposits that require hydraulic fracturing that could be safely exploited. The communities in those regions where natural gas must be fracked would need to apply this analysis to their particular communities' needs and desires and get an idea of what the environmental impact may be.

As we will see in the chapter on Energy, the extraction of any resource in any region is messy and leaves behind some negative impact on the Environment. Economically the process of extraction carries risks and liabilities. These risks and liabilities can outweigh the possible economic benefits of the resource that is extracted.

ISSUE 2: NUCLEAR ENERGY

This is always a sticky Energy source, mostly because it is relatively new in the scale of human achievement and the environmental impacts from radiation are invisible and thus scary. The major Environment impacts are not up front like in hydraulic fracturing but at the end of the process. The scary part is the risk to health and safety, which we will develop later in the discussion on the Economy.

Given this state of affairs, let us at least try and look at nuclear energy with an objective eye and begin with the Environment perspective. How do the polluting externalities of nuclear versus coal power compare and what are the impacts of each on the Natural Environment?

Coal power has an enormous carbon footprint compared to nuclear energy. Coal is basically solid carbon and when burned it releases carbon monoxide, a pollutant and carbon dioxide a greenhouse gas. Unprotected water collects tainted, unhealthy run off from coal extraction operations and from refining and converting processes. Tainted runoff from outdoor stacks of coal or leftover slag can end up in nearby rivers, lakes and streams and can leach into ground water sources if not properly contained and managed. The poisons in water polluted with coal runoff can kill off plants and animals that come into contact with it and can cause birth defects. Expensive pollution control measures are needed to keep the air and water clean from using coal as a fuel and reduce the negative impact on the Natural Environment.

Nuclear energy does not release carbon monoxide or carbon dioxide into the air. For comparison, other Energy sources with low carbon footprints comparable to nuclear are hydroelectric and wind power. But a nuclear power plant does release waste heat that can be carried by steam into the atmosphere or by warm water that is discharged into nearby rivers or cooling ponds. Warm water discharge by riverside nuclear power plants does have an impact on life in the receiving river, especially if the discharge temperature is too high. These high water temperatures can cause algal blooms and disrupt the life cycles of aquatic species of native plants and animals. Fisheries can be destroyed or disrupted.

From a Social Environment perspective how does nuclear energy stack up? This author has lived for over forty years in the shadow of a nuclear power plant. That plant has had no containment issues and no accidents in all the years it has been operating. The nuclear power plant provides steady high paying jobs to engineers and technicians living in the area. New York City gets up to 30% of its electricity from the nuclear power plant. Ask anyone of these stakeholders about the plant and they are happy;

their Family Environment is secure and the communities around the plant get reliable electricity and good jobs.

What a nuclear plant can do that a coal plant cannot is release radiation because of accidents. Radiation can have silent, devastating and long lasting effects on people and nature. But think about how much radiation we are exposing ourselves to just by using cell phones everyday; much more than we get from a nearby nuclear power plant. The radiation risk and other liabilities of nuclear power will be further developed in the Economy chapter.

This discussion gets to two points; talking to the local folks around you and experiencing something first hand has a major impact on one's thinking. It is easy to consider, dismiss or skew an analysis from afar without considering first hand information or experiences. The second point is on keeping the analysis focused with the information at hand and within the framework of our critical thinking. We need always to look for more information at all levels as we move forward and we can add new information later on that may modify or not modify our reasoning and conclusions. It easy to begin jumping right away from the main point of an environmental analysis and being talking about short and long term risks, costs and benefits and so on. So a part of this exercise is also a task in keeping focused. Right now nuclear power is looking very good as an Energy option with respect to the Natural and Social Environments.

ISSUE 3: 10% UNRESTRAINED CORPORATE TAX CUT

Corporate tax cuts are talked about all the time as a solution to all sorts of problems and issues that face us. The thinking over the last thirty years or so goes that giving businesses a no strings attached cut in taxes will fuel job creation and a host of other really good investments. But this is a vastly oversimplified explanation. So hold on a minute and apply the first building block, Environment in our thinking to this problem.

There is great potential for the Natural and Social Environments from an unrestrained corporate tax cut. Take a typical company. Make it any size and have it produce any widgets you want. Supposing that all factors and things that could affect the company's business are stable and in equilibrium; labor costs steady, the market for our company's good or service is good and growing and so on.

Our company owners and executives may take a look at the unrestrained tax cut and decide to register and implement ISO14000, a worldwide environmental standard, with the extra cash. The standard basically says the registered company is a 'greener' company that has recycling programs, good waste management practices and so on. Maybe they invest in equipment that generates less pollution or captures it in such a way so that it has a smaller impact on the Natural Environment. Now the carbon footprint of the company is lower; better for the Natural Environment. The workers are happier because the company does not pollute so much in the neighborhoods that surround the plant in which they live. The company has garnered good will from workers and consumers because its product is seen as environmentally more responsible. Good for the Social Environments the company operates in. All good things for the Natural Environment.

But hold on. We are at the beginning of our review. There are plenty of maybe's out there and no guarantees of good behavior on the part of the company because of the unrestrained tax cut. We can see that every human decision or action does have an impact on the Environment at this point in our exercise but no specific actions have been taken by the company except for no action. What if no action is taken? What if the extra money is not guided towards creating a greener company? Then the positive impact on the Environment is nothing; the status quo. In fact it could be slightly worse than before. Willful ignorance will eventually lead to consumption and decay of scarce resources on the part of the company. And we still need to talk about the potential affects on Energy from our company due to the unrestrained tax cut.

```
E EDUCATION
N
V
I
R            ENERGY: The next concept in our
O ECONOMY    letter 'E'. Our vertical superstruc-
N            ture is in place; the Environment.
M            Now we attach the first horizontal
E            beam, the one that is firm and flat
N            on the ground at the base of the
T E N E R G Y letter 'E' and that is Energy. The
```

reasoning for placing Energy in this position in our critical thinking framework is straightforward enough; to run an Economy you need Energy first, otherwise nothing happens. Trees don't grow in the dark and economies do not run on nothing, power is needed; animal, human, water, the sun whatever the form of Energy there are available, humans use it all. At different times in history the dominant form of Energy we have exploited and consumed has been different; first it was humans and animals, then water and steam power, then electricity, coal, oil and recently on the scale of human history, nuclear.

So we start with the following premise: All forms of Energy extraction, processing and consumption have a negative impact on the Environment. The amount of data and experience covering thousands of years of human civilization bear witness to this conclusion.

Consider the burning of an abundant fuel found all over the world like wood. Cutting down massive numbers of trees reduces the amount of air and water filtering trees do in the Natural Environment. It affects the water cycle, the nitrogen cycle and the carbon cycle adversely. Erosion becomes a huge problem. Benjamin Franklin complained in his day that because all the good wood was gone from the immediate area around Philadelphia folks were forced to travel farther into the countryside to find wood for fuel and for building material, driving up costs. They didn't do tree farming in those days, but Franklin had at least one solution; a better, more efficient stove that used less wood to help keep warm.

So how about coal? Extraction of coal is a messy affair, not to say a heath and safety risk to both the workers and the surrounding Community Environment (note how the Environment already starts to contribute to our thinking about Energy. You will see this time and again in the following discussions. This is why out of the four structural pillars in our critical thinking framework; Environment always comes at the beginning). Think strip mines, tainted water and air pollution from coaling mining and power operations.

Now examine renewable Energy sources starting with wind. It appears to be a very passive source of clean electricity, but some people complain of the aesthetic impact windmills have on a beautiful coastline or mountain top. Other folks in the immediate Community Environment where power windmills are located complain of whining or buzzing noises as the blades spin. It's the sort of annoying noise one hears living next to a high tension power line. Still other folks are concerned with a more direct impact on the Natural Environment and complain of migratory bird kills caused by the spinning blades.

So solar is it. Not really. Acres and acres of solar panels capturing the Sun's rays to provide energy create shade and shadow beneath them. Nothing can grow there, water can not fall on the ground below the panels and a light wind may blow up a dust storm that carries the dry earth into the air and onto the solar panels, thus reducing their efficiency at converting sunlight into electricity.

Given this brief presentation of various forms of Energy, nothing seems to refute the initial premise, so let us consider that Energy consumption and extraction have a negative impact on the Environment as a plain fact. To go further, let us say that selecting and using a source of Energy to fuel human activity is basically a Faustian choice, a 'pick your poison' or whatever other metaphor you chose to use exercise. The question then becomes what is the best choice of Energy with the least amount of negative effects in the Natural Environment that gives the greatest amount of people across all Social Environments the best bang for their buck (the Common Good principle makes its appearance). This obviously leads to considering and using a variety of forms of Energy to run the human affairs on this planet; no one form of Energy can be discounted, tossed aside, not considered or stopped from being used. It is the mix of Energy sources and the scarcity of the resources provided by our Natural Environment as input into the Energy equation we need to consider carefully when assessing the needs and desires of the human population. Consider this as a fact.

Energy extraction and use on this planet are driven by a need; someone needs to cook dinner, a nineteenth century mill needed water power to grind grain, a business needs electricity to make computer chips. Therefore, Energy is very much demand-pull and not so much supply-push. What Energy is demanded is used for a given activity or set of activities at that particular moment; extra Energy sources are not exploited unless someone sees an opportunity to make money on the extraction, refining, conversion or transfer of that Energy based on the market demand.

Before we proceed further in our discussion of Energy it will be instructive to inject a little science; it is fairly easy and when you think about it most of the concepts are common sense based on everyday perception. Energy, which also takes the form of non-useful heat or radiation, is studied through the science of Thermodynamics. It is a big word that in simple terms describes the study of the interaction and relationships between heat and other forms of Energy. Depending on what textbook you reference or scientist one speaks with there are three or four Thermodynamic laws, sometimes one is combined with another or the numbering and order is different; but for the purposes of basic understanding and completeness there are three listed here. So herewith are the laws of Thermodynamics in common layman terms.

1. Energy is always conserved; it cannot be created or destroyed, only change in form. More formally; the internal energy of a system equals the heat plus the work put into it. What this law says is the total amount of Energy in the universe in all its forms is constant. That means the amount of Energy available on Earth is also finite. This is referred to as the Conservation of Energy Law.

2. Law number two states two things; the first being that heat naturally and spontaneously flows from a hot reservoir to a cold one (A refrigerator works in reverse because work and electrical Energy must be used on the system in order to keep your freezer from defrosting and your ice cream from melting. If the electric goes off and someone keeps opening the door – you know what happens) and the second thing being that the randomness or entropy of natural processes left alone is always increasing. Basically this means that in any process of extracting, converting or using Energy to create something or do work, some of the Energy is always wasted usually as heat; nothing is 100% efficient. This is called the Waste or Entropy Law.

3. If two systems A and B are in thermal equilibrium that is, balanced with a third system C, then systems A and B are also in thermal equilibrium with each other. What this basically says is that when things or processes come into contact with each other and interact in some way those things will over time eventually balance out with each other. Think of a basketball balanced on the tip of a cone; hard to do unless you put some work or

Energy into it to keep it from falling off. The ball really wants to be on the floor. Left alone the cone-ball and floor system will reach equilibrium; the cone stays on the floor, the ball falls to the floor, rolls away and comes to a rest someplace. This is the Equilibrium Law.

Basically what these laws say is that the Energy we have available to us here on earth is limited, there is no way to build a perpetual motion machine or build a machine that creates something out of nothing. Although creating a free lunch or the appearance of one is perpetrated quite frequently by politicians, elected officials, Wall Street and businesses with money (not Energy) all the time. It makes one realize that these people, entities and institutions are perhaps not dealing in the real Environment that we all inhabit on a day to day basis.

Think of the three Thermodynamic Laws for a moment and then refer back the discussion on scarcity in the Natural Environment; there is obviously a relationship. The three Laws describe exactly the state of the Natural Environment and well they should.

Rocks fall off hillsides. A ball naturally rolls downhill. Always. Unless someone applies work and pushes the ball back uphill. Glaciers melt when the ambient temperature around them is raised via human and natural activity and stays that way. A glacier will only reform and grow large again if the amount of heat surrounding it everyday becomes less. Once coal is mined from the ground and burned it is gone forever. Electricity is generated to do work elsewhere but the waste heat of combustion never fulfills useful work.

The heat simply vanishes into the atmosphere, is absorbed by ice and liquid water and is radiated into space.

RENEWABLES

Renewable forms of Energy like solar and wind are sometimes called alternative forms of energy but the correct label is probably supplemental energy. If all the solar power that could be developed in our nation was developed and the skies were always sunny, solar still could not replace nuclear power. If the wind blew consistently across the Great Plains, windmills sited there could still not shut down all the coal fired power plants or hydroelectric dams that producing electricity now. That is why it is better to say renewable Energy sources are supplemental forms of Energy.

Both solar and wind power are intermittent sources of Energy. The sun does not shine for 24 hours straight. The wind does not blow all the time. There are sites with a greater amount of sunshine that fall per acre like the southwest of the United States versus the northeast and windier places like the Great Plains or the coastlines but the intermittent nature of solar and wind highlights the fundamental problem each has and that is storage. When the sun does not shine on a photovoltaic cell or the wind stops blowing no power is produced. The collected electricity up to that point must be used immediately or stored somehow for later use. The demand for the electricity is steady. So the electricity or Energy generated from a supplemental Energy source has to be stored in a chemically based battery or in the ground as heat like in a geothermal and solar Energy combination. Batteries and geothermal heat sinks are not very efficient at storing Energy. The chemicals and metals in batteries break down after repeated use. Heat stored in the earth has a habit of dissipating over time. There is a lot of waste, mostly in the form of heat. Storage technology is the limiting factor here as well as the Laws of Thermodynamics.

On the positive side of the ledger, renewable Energy sources have a much lower carbon footprint than traditional sources of Energy like coal or oil. Electricity from a rooftop solar collector does not pump tons of pollutants into the air. The electricity derived from such a setup can be dumped onto the traditional power grid for an Energy credit if it is not being used right away by the home, business or municipality with such a system.

One knock always leveled at solar energy particularly in the northeast part of our nation, is that the sun does not shine often enough or with the right intensity. But Germany receives one third less sunshine on average than the northeast United States and Germany is currently the world leader in the deployment of solar energy.

Wind energy, which is also intermittent, can also be utilized in much the same way as solar by dumping the Energy generated onto the traditional electric grid where it can be transported, taken up and used by someone else who has a demand for it a that particular moment. The electricity can also be stored. Wind Energy scales better than solar; that is, power wind mills can be very large or very small and come with two blades, three blades or more blades, depending on the need, location and the quality and frequency of the wind. Wind can generate a lot of power quickly over a matter of hours or days regardless of whether it is day or night, raining, cloudy or clear skies. But wind is not very predictable; one can generate a wind map with wind speeds that are common in an area or region, but that is no guarantee of future results on a daily demand basis.

The amount of sunshine can be predicted across the same latitudes, but the weather is not very constant and can throw off the amount of Energy you thought could be generated day to day by a solar cell array. Efficiency is also a problem. Solar cells are getting better at converting the sun's rays into electricity but there is still waste from reflection and in the chemical process of conversion. Solar cells obviously only work in the daylight hours and need skies that are clear very often to generate large amounts of electricity.

On the positive side, the costs associated with the manufacturing and construction of wind or solar power stations have come down dramatically in the last several years. Small scale solar or wind installations at households, municipal buildings and warehouse rooftops or at other local levels have become popular and successful in meeting immediate or regional demands for electricity. It is the limitations and cost of storage and the intermittent nature of the Energy sources that hold back both solar and wind from becoming major, principal contributors to our growing demand for cheap and reliable electricity.

ISSUE 1: HYDRAULIC
FRACTURING (FRACKING)

Natural gas is a very clean burning fuel extracted from our Natural Environment. As we are learning, Energy extraction processes can be messy, refining processes can be messy and so can the burning or conversion of fossil fuels to produce power that we humans can then put to productive use. And let us not forget about any waste that is left over at any point in the complete process of producing usable Energy. While Natural gas stores well, burns nicely and leaves manageable waste around after conversion, the natural gas extraction process can prove to be problematic.

A good way to further examine fracked natural gas as an Energy source is by comparing it to other forms of Energy that are available to us. We know that the extraction process of fracking is messy. How about the refining and conversion processes? It turns out that natural gas is mostly methane (chemical notation: CH_4) that is almost immediately available for use as a fuel. But first, moisture needs to be removed from the gas to improve combustion; most natural gas sources are usually associated with underground water so the extra water needs to come out. There are also impurities in the raw gas that need filtering. This refining process is fairly efficient. Except for waste heat and removed water that needs purification before being released back into the Natural Environment, refining is not very messy. Natural gas at this stage can be further refined to make propane or the pure methane gas can be used as a raw feedstock to produce polymers that can be molded and fabricated into auto parts, kitchenware and so on.

The conversion or combustion of natural gas to produce electricity, regardless of the source of the gas is about 50% efficient; much better and cleaner than either burning coal or oil to produce electricity. Coal and oil power plants are efficient in the range of 30% to 40% but not more than 40%. The burning of natural gas produces water vapor and air pollutants like carbon monoxide and carbon dioxide in manageable quantities and produces small quantities of solid particulates, unlike burning coal or oil which are very messy. Think about it; if you have a stove that burns a refined gas like propane does it leave soot all over the kitchen when you cook? How about that open hearth that the colonials cooked over using wood or the coal burning stoves of the nineteenth century? The environmental impact of the natural gas conversion process is minimal and can be managed; the waste products at the end of the conversion process are minimal and can be controlled. There is no question about it, natural gas, regardless of the source, when looked at from refining through conversion in the Energy production process is a clean and efficient source or Energy. It is just that big mess at the very beginning; the extraction of the natural resource, the externality of the potential pollution of a watershed that supplies fresh water to millions of people that overshadows fracking operations. This is our major source of concern.

Do we need to be extracting natural gas from the earth with hydraulic fracturing? Is there truly a huge demand now to use this resource for electricity production? Must fracking occur within the greater Catskill Region? Is it profitable? With or without a subsidy? From an environmental risk standpoint, fracking for gas in the Delaware Watershed area is still problematic for all the affected parties both on site and downstream. Clean water is still more important. Looked at from an Energy perspective, natural gas extracted by fracking or any other operation presents less of carbon footprint during conversion compared to coal or oil and produces less waste afterwards that is more manageable. We will continue our examination of hydraulic fractured natural gas in our discussion of the Economy.

ISSUE 2: NUCLEAR ENERGY

Nuclear energy is based on an atomic reaction using a fuel that is naturally occurring. Nuclear power plants use Uranium, Boron, Silver and Carbon that are mined from the ground, refined and reacted together to produce electricity. There is waste at each point of the process; so where do we find the mess and the wastes of most concern in the nuclear energy process? How does nuclear energy stack up against other forms of Energy?

First look at the extraction process. Uranium has to mined from the ground like coal. Uranium as a naturally occurring substance in the ground is not concentrated and is combined with other rocks and elements and is only weakly radioactive in this raw form and not useful as a fuel at this point. Mining for Uranium is not unlike mining for coal. Mining has been around for thousands of years; humans know how to do it and the risks are well known. Unlike coal however, Uranium is not often found near the surface and is not strip mined like coal can be. Water tainted by coal mining operations is far more dangerous and toxic to humans that water tainted by raw Uranium. The air in or around a mine, particularly a strip mine is unhealthy, no matter what you are digging for. So as far as waste in the extraction process, Uranium is not unlike any other fuel source found in the ground and may on balance be slightly cleaner during extraction since it is not strip mined like coal. And the mining of Uranium is highly regulated by the government. Uranium mining may have slightly less adverse impact on our Natural and Social Environments compared to coal extraction.

How about waste in refining? Uranium also comes out ahead of coal. Uranium refining is done under very regulated, controlled lab like conditions in order to concentrate the radioactive isotopes and make the raw Uranium into yellow cake, the next form the material takes on before it can become useable in a nuclear reactor. Or a bomb. The raw material is mechanically crushed to make the yellow cake powder, then it is exposed to fluoride gas in a process called gas diffusion but it is still not radioactive enough for use. This low enriched Uranium is put in a centrifuge until enough U235 Uranium radioactive isotope is concentrated for use as fuel. After this step it is usually made into cylindrical pellets like wood pellets that can be stacked together in a nuclear reactor fuel rod.

What you do not see is great heaps of Uranium lying out in the open exposed to the Natural Environment, unlike freshly mined coal which is left in huge piles exposed to the elements. When it rains, runoff from coal piles ends up in someone's water supply. While the bomb making aspect of Uranium refining is scary, the refining process is far more controlled and less wasteful than any sort of coal refining; if any refining is done at all to the coal besides crushing it into useful chunks. Scariness does not qualify as waste.

But it does hint at the risk and potential future liabilities of nuclear power.

Next we look at the actual process of creating electricity from a controlled nuclear fission reaction. The little pellets are still mildly radioactive at this point. They need to be stacked on top of each other in a rod and then the rods must be bundled closely together to get a nuclear fission reaction going. In a fission reaction, the atoms actually split apart, producing a lot of Energy from a small amount of material. This is where the Silver and Boron come in. Without other rods containing mostly Silver or Boron (there are other elements that can be used as well) surrounding the hot uranium rods, the reactor would just go wild, melt down and release harmful radiation. What the other materials do is absorb neutrons from the nuclear reaction and control that reaction, so that the heat produced can actually be harnessed and turned into useful work. The heat of the nuclear reaction is used to turn water into steam, which in turn drives a turbine to produce electricity. None of this radioactive 'hot' water ever gets out into the Environment. Only outside water taken in from a nearby water source that is used to cool the hot inside steam back into liquid water again through a heat exchanger is discharged back into the external Natural Environment. In this sense, a nuclear reactor is a closed system with only the exchange of heat going on between the radioactive water inside the power plant and the cooling water from the outside Environment.

Coal burning produces waste heat as well. The coal is burned to make steam to drive a turbine to make electricity. This waste heat usually goes up a smokestack or into a body of water. The amount of discharged heat between coal and nuclear during conversion to electricity is similar (the water used to drive the steam turbines has to be brought up to the same temperature and pressure since the turbines used in both coal and nuclear power are really no different in design and performance) if you are comparing facilities with the same power generation ratings. Without getting too scientific, water is used in both processes and water the world over has the same specific heat or capacity to absorb and discharge heat no matter what process injects the heat into it. Air has a different specific heat, is less dense and you need more of it to absorb the same amount of heat, but in the end the heat is the heat that is discharged into the Natural Environment from similarly rated power plants.

Again, depending on the sources you review, typical coal plants are about 30% to 35% efficient in producing electricity, about the same as a nuclear reactor. Some new coal plant designs claim over 40% efficiency with new supercritical boilers and turbines and some new reactor designs can claim this efficiency as well. So as far as examining the waste heat from the conversion of both fuels to usable Energy, nuclear and coal are basically the same.

With respect to supplemental energy forms like solar and wind, nuclear power is steady, more reliable and more efficient than any renewable source of Energy. You get a big supply of Energy from nuclear power regardless of the weather or time of day. The only fuel that converts cleaner to usable Energy is natural gas.

But now we are at the end; the nuclear fuel is spent. All the fission that can occur has occurred. What to do with the spend fuel rods? This is the interesting part of the Energy analysis between nuclear, coal, natural gas and any other fuel source for that matter. The Environmental assessment of nuclear waste can be scary and the whole process of nuclear waste processing and containment is highly regulated.

A spent fuel rod must be collected from the reactor and stored. Spent fuel usually spends time in a cool down pool filled with water inside the reactor vessel at the reactor site. Then it is carefully moved and mixed with other inert materials and finally stored in a sarcophagus made of cement and steel. The radiation from spent fuel stored in this manner is so low and the containment so safe that one nuclear power worker this author has spoken to has gone so far to say that he would gladly store the sarcophagus in his backyard. Now think about this; everyday we are zapping more radiation directly into our heads with cell phones than we will ever be exposed to from a nuclear power plant operation.

The problem is that we are running out of room at the reactor sites to store this waste. It has to go somewhere secure and safe. Safe places have been proposed and found but nothing has been agreed on. But now go back and look at the entire nuclear Energy process. If we agree on what to do with the waste at the end we get to use an efficient fuel to generate electricity. It is too soon to decide to throw nuclear power out of our energy mix.

With respect to the Natural and Social Environments and Energy production, nuclear power looks like a far better option than any other form of Energy available to us, be it traditional fossil fuels or renewables. The carbon footprint of nuclear energy is less than other forms of Energy; pollution is less; the conversion process is robust. It is the risks out there in the future particularly with regards to waste and to the security of the refining process that need to be addressed. In our Economy discussion we will come back to the risks associated with Uranium refining and the storage of nuclear waste and what can be done to address these concerns.

ISSUE 3: 10% UNRESTRAINED CORPORATE TAX CUT

So far, our 10% unconstrained corporate tax cut has held up under Environmental and Energy scrutiny. But the supposed benefits or lack thereof are in the abstract. They are hypothetical. Our Environmental analysis so far has includes a lot of 'buts,' 'maybes,' and other conditionals.

Is there an Energy perspective to investigate? Sure there is. Any business needs Energy to run; even labor represents a form of Energy, in particular human energy. Energy is a necessary and required input into their economic activity. So suppose all things on the supplier side are in a state or in Equilibrium; labor costs are steady, the cost of electricity is steady no new competitors have entered the market. These are big assumptions but let us move forward. Our company is feeling pretty good. That 10% unrestrained tax cut could be used for positive benefits. Maybe our company can implement the ISO14000 Environmental standard. To do this, it basically takes setting up and implementing processes like paper recycling, energy saving strategies, more efficient transport and storage operations and waste management protocols; in essence creating a 'greener' more efficient running company. This sounds pretty good. Maybe the company can use the money the government has returned to them to put solar panels on its rooftops to supplement their traditional Energy sources and lower the company carbon footprint. Pollution may be reduced as a result of these Energy saving efforts. This tax cut could really have a positive impact on Energy consumption and the Environment. But we still have too many maybes.

E EDUCATION
N
V
I
R   **THE ECONOMY** is the middle
O ECONOMY   beam in our letter 'E'. As we have
N   seen, a health Economy very much
M   depends on a healthy Environment
E   and a reasonable mix and avail-
N   ability of reliable Energy to run
T E N E R G Y properly and successfully for long

periods of time. An Economy consists of all the trade, dis-
tribution and consumption of goods and services in a given
region using available capital, labor and natural resources.
The exchange of those goods and services is based on the
supply and demand between market participants in that
Economy.

SUPPLY AND DEMAND

Adam Smith laid out the fundamentals of Economic
thought in *The Wealth of Nations* published in 1776. The
basic premise in Smith's book is that all human commerce
depends on the supply and the demand for goods or services in a marketplace. To demonstrate; sometime at the
turn of the 20th century...I live in New York City and I
need to keep my milk and eggs fresh so I need ice for my
new ice box. Especially in summer. There is a grocer with

ice up the block, but I have to carry it myself to the apartment and it is big and heavy. Now there are more people moving into the neighborhood and more folks want ice for their new ice boxes. I don't want to have to start paying more or going further away from my home to get ice. This is the demand side. On the supply side; I have a small carting business in New York City. I carry fruit and vegetables around to the different groceries. Lately folks are complaining about the price of ice for their ice boxes. And they have to carry it home themselves. What if I make a deal with an ice company upstate? I'll take advance orders, and when the ice comes down on the steamer, I'll pick it up and deliver it door to door to customers. And I think I can do it cheaper than the grocer up the street. Maybe I can pay off my initial investment in labor and capital goods and make still more money by expanding the service to more neighborhoods. What if other guys get into the business after I do? This is the supply side. Of course what we have also demonstrated on the supply side is the profit motive. The motive of any business is to make money; a principal human desire occasionally known as greed in its excessive forms.

In order to demonstrate the concept of supply and demand more clearly, refer to the following graph and memorize it.

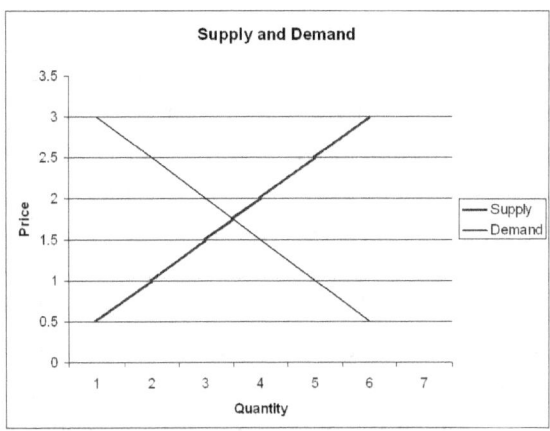

Everyone at some point, whether in a high school class on Economics or at the college level has seen this graph and if not then woe to the Education system because everyone should have come across it in their studies. This graph describes human commerce at the basic level; supply and demand, profit motive, needs and desires and risk. One can do some very good, basic economic analysis with this graph. Let us go through the graph so that we have a good understanding of all the components that make it up.

The graph has two axes; a vertical axis labeled 'price' and a horizontal axis labeled 'quantity.' There are two intersecting lines on the chart; the line sloping from the upper left to the lower right represents the *demand* for a good or service and the line sloping from lower left to upper right represents the *supply* of a good or service.

The Law of Demand basically states that all else being equal the demand or quantity asked for a good or service declines as the price increases. This is easy to see on the graph and is common sense to anyone who buys groceries or any other item on the open market. If something is too expensive you don't buy much of it; if the good or service you desire as the buyer is cheap you want to buy more of it. Hey! Apples are on sale now…lets stock up.

The Law of Supply states that everything else being equal, the higher the price the more quantity of a good or service is supplied. This is true because sellers like small businesses and large corporations know that selling more of something at a higher price means more revenue and potentially more profit. Supply is driven very much by time since a supplier may not be able to react quickly enough to changes in demand for a good or service. Hey! I have plenty of apples in cold storage and that sale has been going on for a week now and I didn't know about it! My competitor beat me to the market.

Where the demand and supply lines intersect is the *equilibrium* point. Refer back to our discussion in Energy about equilibrium and you will immediately see a parallel to supply and demand in the Economy. The equilibrium point on the supply and demand graph represents the point at which a given good or service is delivered most efficiently to market. The amount of the good or service demanded exactly equals what is supplied. If you draw a horizontal line from the intersection point to the price axis you get the equilibrium price. If you draw a vertical line from the intersection point to the quantity axis you get the equilibrium quantity.

This is a dynamic graph; that is the demand line can be shifted left or right. A shift in the demand line to the right indicates a demand for a greater quantity of a good or service. Factors that can shift the demand line left or right are consumer incomes, population shifts, availability of other similar goods and services and changing consumer preferences. For example, an increase in demand could be represented as an increase in the demand for clean water to meet the needs a growing human population in a particular region of the world; it could represent an increase in consumer demand for electricity or a natural resource like oil as people demand better shelter with more conveniences and appliances that need power to run.

The supply curve can be shifted left or right. A shift in the supply line indicates a change in the quantity supplied of a good or service. The supply line can be shifted by the number of competitors entering or leaving a market, by technology, the price of inputs to produce the good or service, or the price of other similar goods and services. A leftward shift of the supply line indicates a scarcity or an increased cost of an input to the supplier; like a natural resource suddenly becoming harder to find that is used to produce the good or service. Maybe natural gas that was easy to extract and drill for previously with an old, proven technology is getting scarce. Electricity generated from natural gas is now more expensive. There is less natural gas around to use as feedstock to make basic plastics. A supplier now has higher Energy costs to produce plastic bowls, automobile parts or keep the lights on in his business offices.

Stop for a moment. It should be clear at this point that there is a logical order to our Environment, Economy,

Energy and Education critical thinking framework. Energy is an input into the supply side of Economic activity. Energy has to come before Economics otherwise no economic activity can take place. Energy has to come from some resource. The resources to generate Energy are found in the Environment. So Environment must come before Energy. A simple, direct and logical progression of our critical thinking tools.

It should also be noted that both the demand and supply lines can be moved simultaneously to get a new equilibrium point between price and quantity for a given good or service. Given the sly examples introduced here to illustrate the shifting of the supply and demand curves, the reader can see this graph is a powerful and simple tool that can be used to analyze the economic affects of utilizing scarce natural resources present in our Environment, the impact of using those natural resources to meet our Energy requirements, the effect of buying more locally grown food on our Community Environment, the availability of good teachers in Education and so forth.

Anyone wishing to study supply and demand further is not lacking in any references; a simple internet search on supply and demand will turn up hundreds of images and text on the subject.

THE ZOG PRINCIPLE

There is no better way to describe this idea other than with cavemen. Thousands of years ago, cavemen had a basic understanding of economics and the human motivations behind creating an economy. Way back when in the early days of modern humanity, there was Zog the caveman. Zog ran a small hunting party, employing other able men in his tribe to go out and hunt for meat and skins. Zog and his party went into the field and collected ten skins and brought them back to his tribe. The Chieftain always took two skins, after all he was the Chief. Zog didn't like it but it was for the Common Good of the tribe. But suppose that after collecting the ten skins, the Chieftain tells Zog that because of the particularly high number of new children born and a sniff in the air that tells him that a harsh winter is in store for the tribe, Zog must give him three skins. Sure Zog is pissed, but for the next hunting trip he finds a few more young cavemen to hire and go farther afield with him to hunt with the promise of payment after the hunt. They succeed and bring back fourteen skins. Not only did Zog make up for the lost skin to the Chieftain he had extra skins to pay for the new guys in his party.

Now suppose the Chieftain instead tells Zog that because he is such a great caveman, instead of taking an extra skin he is going to give on back. What do you think Zog is going to do? Certainly not hire extra cavemen to hunt better. He won't travel further out into the hunting grounds. He doesn't need to. Instead Zog will take the extra skin and blow it on something unproductive like the Mastodon races.

An astute reader will have already noted in this amusing example what is being presented; *incentives* and the *profit motive* go a long way toward the hiring of labor or the creation of new products and services that have value and benefit to the Common Good in this case, Zog and his tribe. The extra skin the Chieftain wants is a tax increase, nobody likes it, especially a businessman like Zog but it is an incentive that works all too well and has worked all too well throughout American history after panics and recessions.

When the incentive or motivator of the extra missing skin is lifted with no strings attached; when the Chief gives Zog back a skin for no particular reason and for not wanting anything in particular in return, this is an unrestrained tax cut. Zog has no incentive to do more hunting or hire more hunters, although he may make vague promises about it and never really follow through on any of them. This is the basic problem with implementing some aspects of supply side economics. The results of implementing trickle down supply side theory on and off over the last thirty years or so are at best mixed. Tax cuts or credits without conditions or constraints do not necessarily drive business to do what you would want them to do, that is hire more people, or pay them more or invent new products or services.

There is nothing wrong with supply side theory; it has been the implementation that has fallen short of the premise. All accountability on business has been removed. Results have not been linked to performance or expectations. Zog has been away at the races. Wealth has become more concentrated at the top. Therefore, success with business tax cuts can only occur with reasonable conditions attached. A proper implementation of business tax cuts will include constraints or conditions designed to create incentives and produce the desired positive results for the Common Good. Like creating jobs.

RISK

Any study of Economics needs to include a discussion on risk. At the heart of every transaction for goods and services there is risk. Risk has the ability to move the supply and demand lines. Risk on the demand side has an influence on consumer preferences. As a consumer one can think; am I paying a fair price for these apples? What if there is a comparable good or service available for less that will satisfy my needs? Pears are in season now and they are locally grown, maybe I will purchase pears instead.

For a business risk has an affect on the cost on inputs. What if I switch to or buy more renewable Energy to keep my lights on? What if the price of electricity from a traditional source like a coal power plant suddenly drops? Will this investment I made in labor and capital to put solar panels on my roof payoff or will I loose my investment? What if my good or service causes harm to the buyer? My cold storage apples have been sitting around for a year, are they still edible? Is this a good time to enter the market?

But risk is not always uniform in its application. The consumer population may be captive; I need internet access and I only have one cable provider right now. What if this new DSL service is really slow or does not work? I have to cancel my old service first before the new service will even come out to take a look at the pole in front of my house and see if they can give me service, and I have to pay up front. The switching costs are pretty high, especially if the new service doesn't work and I have to go back to the old provider. The hell with it, I'll stay with my existing service even if I'm not totally happy with it.

For a business; Hey! There is no one in the market right now with a really good portable digital music player. Great! I can be first in and probably get a nice return on investment. My digital music player does not even have to be that great, just work acceptably for a reasonable amount of time. The cost of entry is not that great since the technology exists to make such a music player. All I need to do is put the pieces together in a nice package and market it.

When looking at and assessing a problem or issue from an economic standpoint, understanding risk or the motivation behind doing something or not doing something is important. In other words, try and walk a mile in the other person's moccasins during any part of your analysis.

EXTERNALITIES

An externality is generally defined as the unintended consequences of human activity. An externality can have positive or negative impacts. The unintended consequence of a baseball game played before a live audience is that the people in attendance enjoy it. The players also get exercise but the real economic intention is to sell tickets, peanuts and beer and make money. Your neighbor may plant some very beautiful roses by the roadside; the flowers hang over the garden wall. Even though the rose garden is intended for her enjoyment, the unintended consequence is that passersby including you can enjoy the smell and look of the roses as well. Your neighbor paid for all the gardening supplies and put in the time to cultivate the roses but the passersby paid nothing for the benefit they receive from the well tended garden.

Externalities can also have negative consequences as well. Businesses do not deal very well with negative market externalities like pollution caused by their operations. Here are a couple of examples that illustrate bad market externalities and the attitude of the companies that caused them. More than forty years ago an automotive company had a plant in northern New Jersey. The area is surrounded by woods and the Ramapo Mountains. There were not too many regulations regarding industrial waste back then and little oversight. Not many people lived in the area. So the company simply filled up trucks with old sticky paint contaminated with carcinogenic substances harmful to humans, plants and other animals and dumped it down old mine shafts where the mess continues to pollute the local water supply. It is hard to clean up. Many years later, the company has taken responsibility and settled with residents but it has been the government and tax dollars that have mostly been used to remediate the old paint problem for the good of the people and the Environment harmed by the pollution.

Another more famous example of water pollution happened nearby in the Hudson River. General Electric had a plant way upstate that discharged PCBs, a very harmful chemical, into the Hudson where it was allowed to trickle downstream. Tides and current swished the foul mess back and forth and mixed it with the mud and silt in the water. Some PCBs were flushed out into the ocean, some of it settled with the mud onto the river bottom. After years of dragging their feet General Electric has agreed to pay for some dredging and clean up costs. But the corporate delays had the intended effect; after forty or so years the harmful chemicals have been captured in a layer of mud under the Hudson River, undisturbed as so many more layers of mud have been added on top. Over time, the Environment has forcefully but slowly been fixing this mess caused by irresponsible humans.

These two examples should clearly illustrate the typical corporate attitude to market externalities. Ignore and don't deal with it. Someone else will pay for the cleanup; the someone else usually being an unsuspecting public.

Guided by the principle that every human decision and activity has an impact on the Environment, it is important to note all the causes and effects of that decision or activity up front. Be aware of the market externalities; do not try to hide them and clearly assess the risks or rewards of the decision or activity. This is an essential part of critical thinking and analysis. Our framework of Environment, Energy, Economy and Education helps to reveal and assess all sides of an issue and keeps externalities and risks squarely in view and accounted for.

SUBSIDIES

The subsidizing of various human activities is an attempt to create an artificial boost to demand or cost support for supply in an Economy. Subsidies can be monetary in nature or use labor or capital at below the market cost to support the activity. Not all subsidies come from the government, but many do. Many subsidies end up benefiting a few entities or individuals. Take subsidies for supplemental or renewable energy sources like wind and solar. In the long term the supplemental Energy source being subsidized may benefit the Common Good but in the short term it is using a scarce resource, public money, to prop it up. The demand is supported by offering installation tax credits to those who want to use solar or wind power and the supply side is helped by offering incentives to manufacturers to make solar panels and wind turbines. Now look at oil and gas subsidies. Hydraulic fracturing for natural gas gets a subsidy. Oil and gas companies are some of the most profitable companies on the face of the earth; so why are we subsidizing them for this activity?

Think of the ethanol subsidies given to the corn farmers in our nation. Ethanol derived from corn has a high per unit extraction and refining price, slightly higher than the actual value of the Energy derived from the finished product. Ethanol derived from sugar cane on the other hand, has a positive per unit energy value when taking into account its extraction and refining costs. But we don't grow much sugar cane in the United States. Brazil does. So does it make sense to subsidize ethanol derived from corn grown by a few large domestic farmers versus simply purchasing ethanol on the open market even if it may come from Brazil? It is probably cheaper to do away with the subsidy and go to the open market for ethanol.

Now look at electricity from solar Energy. There are a couple ways to go; direct conversion with photovoltaic cells or indirectly by converting water into steam to run a turbine. We have already noted some of the environmental downsides and upsides to solar Energy. Unfortunately, neither of these methods of creating usable Energy from the

Sun is very efficient or cost effective on a large scale. Again the profit motive of business would have already created a heavy investment in solar Energy if there was money to be made in the activity. It may prove upon further examination that smaller scale rooftop photovoltaic cell installations are much more viable economically as a supplement to traditional Energy sources. If home or small business solar Energy production does take off and become widely implemented, then the subsidies for it may be reduced or eliminated over time. This small scale implementation of solar Energy is a local Social Environment solution, and it certainly appears more viable at the present time than large scale solar Energy installations.

This is not to say that all subsidies are bad. In some cases young industries need a boost to over come high startup costs or demand needs a kick start. In other cases, trade competitors on the world market for goods or services provide subsidies to their businesses at the expense of similar businesses in our nation, taking advantage of our free trade stance. A level playing field is required. In the case of green Energy a sound argument can be made that a subsidy for solar or wind Energy creates domestic manufacturing jobs in several Community and Regional Environments around our nation. A subsidy may make us less dependent on foreign sources of Energy and thus more secure economically. In this case and others the Common Good principle takes affect.

But the application of a subsidy for a particular business, commodity or Energy source must be analyzed very carefully in scope and in detail, something that the reader should be able to do upon reading and understanding the concepts in this small volume on critical thinking. It may be a good idea to consider sunset clauses or expiration dates for subsidies with renewal or extension of the subsidy contingent upon the success or failure of the good or service being subsidized. The impact the subsidy has on scarce resources and tax dollars must be considered. A basic, truthful analysis can be done with our principles and four 'E' critical thinking tools to come up with a reasonable answer on whether to start a subsidy or continue to subsidize or not.

A WORD ON GOVERNMENT

Government is not evil, nor does it have to burdensome. When there are two major opposing forces in a system, like capital (business) and labor in an Economy, rules are established and a referee selected to enforce the rules that guide the activity between the opposing forces. Government is the referee; the guarantor of the laws, rules and regulations that are agreed upon by the interested parties.

Think of a football game without officials. One team eventually will win and it will be a lopsided win. Why? Because the team that cheats first will gain clear unfair advantages over their rivals quickly. Maybe they will illegally hold the other players on the line of scrimmage more often or start clothes lining the quarterback. Maybe those passes to the sidelines were all out of bounds. Maybe the owner of the team has more money than all the other owners in the league and will simply buy all the best players for his team at the expense of everyone else. So what? There are no officials to govern the game. The shrewdest most unfair team wins all the time.

Unfettered economic activity or commerce run amok in a totally free market without reasonable regulations and checks and balances on the activities of the participants leads to a rapid depletion of scarce resources, high human misery and the concentration of wealth; in other words a lopsided victory. Think about the middle ages and feudalism.

Government exits to make sure market externalities like pollution or health risks are dealt with fairly by all parties and stakeholders. The government has been established and empowered by the people. Government makes sure there is a level playing field for economic activity and that the rules established and agreed to by all parties guiding that activity are followed. In our republic system of government one side or the other, labor or business, will occasionally gain an unfair advantage because of a bad call or series of bad calls by government. But there are correcting mechanisms like voting and the courts in place to check the excesses of power, money and the masses. The corrections may not be felt immediately but they will take affect. Trust the government, check it from time to time and make adjustments as necessary to ensure fairness for all the players.

ISSUE 1: HYDRAULIC FRACTURING (FRACKING)

So far hydraulic fracturing for natural gas, at least in the greater Catskill and New York City Regions is not a very good idea with respect to the Natural Environment and the Social Environments involved. Let us take a look at this from an Economic perspective and see how our answer evolves.

The very first thing that comes to mind is demand for natural gas. Empirically and through common experience there is a regular demand pull for this natural resource to produce electricity and also to produce products made of plastic. The demand for natural gas is not going to go away overnight. Consumer electricity demand is still there and increasing. The power plants that use natural gas are still standing and need fuel to run.

How about the supply side? What is cost of inputs versus the potential return on investment of a hydraulic fracturing operation? The inputs are basic; a geological survey, land, water under pressure, sand, chemicals, some basic equipment like a portable drilling rig and a tanker truck, and a few people to run the local operation. The cost of traditional extraction methods is lower compared to the new method of hydraulic fracturing but traditional natural gas supplies are running out. Once a natural resource runs out it is gone regardless of how cheap the traditional method of extraction is, there is nothing left to extract. Time to leave the old market and enter a new one.

So we ask more questions. How long has the average fracking well been productive? It is turns out only a few months to a few years on average, not the twenty or so years the industry first estimated to make the wells appear profitable. Therefore, more hydraulic fracturing wells must be drilled in a concentrated area over a shorter span of time. It also turns out that any profitability from fracking is supported by a subsidy.

What about the earnings of the landowners from gas leases? The gas extraction companies generally will not let the landowner keep more than a 12% share. What happens to the rest of the shares? The gas extraction company sells the remaining shares on the open market before even one cubic meter of gas is extracted, generating profits from the sale of the shares that accrue only to the gas extraction company. Once the gas is extracted, the gas company will not sell it right away; rather it is stored until peak demand conditions exist to sell it on the market for good profit. The profit accrues to the gas company and the gas company only. The landowner sees none of these secondary profits; in addition the leases often do not compensate the landowner for crop loss, timber loss or water contamination. Insurance companies are demanding high property coverage premiums from landowners that have gas leases because of the liabilities and risks involved with hydraulic fracturing.

So, for a little bit of up front money the landowner is on the hook for enormous risks. This does not look like a fair tradeoff; there is no equilibrium between the land owner and the gas extraction company. The majority of profits do not trickle down to the local Social Environment. The major economic benefits of fracking for natural gas appear to accrue to only a few business owners and investors. In the old days of oil exploration, this was known as wildcatting.

The job perspective in a case like this is also always overstated. The number of jobs provided or saved in the local Social Environment, for example in Pennsylvania where hydraulic fracturing for natural gas is occurring, has never met the goal of hundreds of thousands of jobs projected for the region.

From this economic perspective hydraulic fracturing for natural gas is probably a break even proposition at best looking at the input costs, the subsidies and the risks versus the monetary returns from demand of the product. The containment of water pollution and other risks associated with the process of fracking for natural gas do not appear to have been taken seriously or factored into any long range economic assessment. These risks are being passed down to local landowners who do not see much of the profits. That is, any clean up, remediation or compensation due to negative externalities to the landowners or end users of the fresh water or natural gas derived from the greater Catskill region are assumed to be borne by the government and the public. The hidden costs will be taken up by the various affected Social Environments and any mess leftover absorbed by the Natural Environment long after fracking operations have ceased and the owners and investors in the fracking operations have walked away with profits. The few gaining at the expense of the many; a violation of the principle of the Common Good. Poor John Adams.

ISSUE 2: NUCLEAR ENERGY

From an economic perspective, closing all the existing nuclear power plants and not building new ones has the effect of shutting down the Economy. The demand pull for electricity is steady and is not declining. Consumers want more power. The human population is growing. The demand line is shifting to the right on our graph. The constant focus and all the impulsive talk about the health and safety of the Natural and Social Environments surrounding a nuclear power plant can be scary. But it merely avoids dealing rationally and pragmatically with the risks, benefits and externalities associated with nuclear Energy. So let us face our fears head on and up front.

Consider and acknowledge the three most notorious nuclear accidents; Three Mile Island, Chernobyl, Fukushima. The first two were the result of human action or inaction, the third caused by a natural environmental act and the human failure to account for that act in the plant design from the very beginning. No one lost a life from Three Mile Island, the only domestic failure of a nuclear power plant. The other two failed in the gravest way possible; a melt down. The melt downs were devastating to the Regional, Community and Family Social Environments they served, supported and were located in as well as to the surrounding Natural Environment. The situations continue to be monitored in the most serious way. Clean up is still occurring.

Now consider how other nations handle the risk of nuclear power, like France. Nuclear power is the principal source of electricity for our French friends. They understand it, live near it and are fully aware of the risks. They have had no major accidents. You mean to tell me that the French are better at handling highly sophisticated technology than Americans? That over fifty years of safe nuclear reactor operation in our nation means nothing? There are two things to point out here; the first is an irrational assessment of economic risk concerning nuclear power and secondly unwillingness on the part of some stake-holders to face the real safety and health issues associated with an Energy source. More people have died in plane crashes and car accidents over fifty years than have died from nuclear power accidents. More people have died in coal mining accidents and from black lung than from leak-ing radiation. Cell phone radiation is frying our brains not nuclear power. More Natural Environments have been permanently scarred by strip mining operations, coal fires and tainted runoff water from coal power operations than have been marred by nuclear power. Fear of nuclear power should not rule the day. That is no way to run a railroad. So let us cut through the distractions with more rational and pragmatic thinking about nuclear power.

Consider Bikini Atoll, the site of many nuclear test explosions. A small population of islanders was moved to safer grounds before the tests. One test used old warships anchored around the lagoon. The test sank an old aircraft carrier that was bent by the huge wave that followed the blast. The sunken wrecks were and remained highly radio-active after the blast. No one was allowed to Bikini for a very long time. The Islanders have been kept away for safety; the government ended up monetarily compensating them for the loss of their homeland. Cut to sixty years later. The lingering radiation has decreased to safe levels. Marine life swims around and encrusts the old wrecks. Sea water has carried away and dissipated some of the radioactivity. It acts as an insulator. The old wrecks are now destinations for scuba diving enthusiasts. Our government through all the passage of time and administrations has acted in a responsible way with respect to the Bikini nuclear tests.

Now to the waste part. Nuclear waste is a market externality with risk that must be dealt with safely and rationally. Regulations dictate how it is to be stored and managed. But the storage is now mostly occurring at the power stations themselves. It all needs to go somewhere safe. Like the deepest parts of the ocean. Or underground, like under a mountain. Yucca Mountain in Nevada has been proposed as a nuclear waste repository and the proposal was moving forward until recently. Many people in that state and outside of it are not fond of the idea so the work on the repository has been stopped. But once again the needs of the Common Good should take precedence. The methods of storage, handling and management of nuclear waste are well understood and regulated so why not Yucca Mountain? The population in the area is scattered. Why does the government simply say it goes under the mountain and be done with it? There are many non rational reasons including fear that have halted the project.

Remain calm, think rationally and consider the Common Good. Think Eisenhower Interstate Highway System. It is a grand system of cross country road transportation that has greatly supported and enhanced economic activity in the country for decades. This highway system is the spine of cross country commerce that our grandfathers had the forethought to build for the ultimate benefit of future generations. Think of the hundreds of displaced families, destroyed or relocated communities, plowed under arable and productive farmland and miles of rivers that were spanned, dammed and redirected to build this immense project. Now Yucca Mountain or something like it does not look like so much of a problem for storing nuclear waste. Why are we letting our irrational fears hold up a project of national importance?

Nuclear energy highlights both economic risk and economic externalities in grand fashion. The point being is that, even though the passage of time mitigated the radioactive circumstances of Bikini Island, even though Chernobyl melted down the situations were isolated and handled with all possible swiftness by government. Yes, that government. In fact our government has the world over, through our public funds kept nuclear material safe, the nuclear Energy extraction and refining processes safe and the operation of nuclear power plants regulated with maximum benefit to the Economy, all Social Environments and with the least impact on the Natural Environment. We have enjoyed the safe delivery and use of reliable electricity generated by nuclear energy to the Economy for over fifty years. A pretty good track record, given the present and future risks of this source of Energy. We know the risks very well. We take them seriously and they are factored into our planning for nuclear energy. Fear has not ruled the day, instead reasonable minds have held sway.

There simply is no way that nuclear energy can be taken completely off the table. Given the will of the nation, the economic demand for Energy, the scarcity of other resources and the much greater negative impact of other forms of Energy on the Environment, nuclear energy is hear to stay and must be a part of any Energy mix we envision to meet the needs of a growing and more sophisticated human population.

ISSUE 3: 10% UNRESTRAINED CORPORATE TAX CUT

The unrestrained tax cut survives our Energy scrutiny, but does it? The gorilla in the bedroom that no one wants to address with regards to this tax cut idea is the 'unrestrained' part. Politicians and shrewd businessmen present the tax cut so simply it is easy to buy into. Cut corporate taxes, create jobs and investment opportunities. But now we know the Zog Principle. Just handing 10% of the tax money already being collected back to corporations with no strings attached is like giving back the skin free and clear to Zog. There is *no guarantee* that the company will do anything productive or constructive with the *free* money. A corporate tax cut can help a company deal responsibly with messy market externalities like pollution created by company operations. The Natural Environment the company resides in could be cleaner. A company could lower its carbon footprint with investments in clean energy or pollution control technology. The company can garner much good will by becoming a greener functioning company in the Social Environments it sells its goods or services in.

However, our hypothetical environmental improvements will likely never happen for a number of reasons. The steady economic state we assumed for the company is rarely the state of affairs for any going concern. Energy costs are on the rise. Labor costs fluctuate; what if a local governor abolishes trade unions where the company has operations? What if the company moves operations to a country with lower labor costs? Sadly for labor in this nation, many of these things have happened and continue to happen. Now the company's cost of inputs, specifically labor is much lower than before. Who cares about all that environmental stuff now? Why invest in pollution control devices and environmental standards? The company may not invest in cleaner Energy solutions; it has no incentive to do so. It probably will not lower its carbon footprint. Companies are in business to make a profit; they do not directly care about your health, safety or economic condition or externalities that can make operations more costly or hurt profitability. An externality like free ranging air pollution is not their problem; pollution effects and costs are shoved off onto the public and the government.

Imagine you are walking with a traffic light across the street in a well lit and marked crosswalk. Someone runs the red light, hits you and drives on. The driver is identified. But you are held 100% liable for all your medical and recovery costs. The driver pays nothing. Fair? Of course not. But this is what companies do everyday; pass unsightly costs and damages to society. They simply have no incentive with the unrestrained tax cut to hire anyone, invest in new products or services or help manage any pollution they may cause from operations. A 10% Unrestrained Corporate Tax Cut? A bad idea. Violates the Zog Principle and neglects the negative impact of human decisions on the Natural and Social Environments. Cause and effect is thrown out the window. The interrelation of activities is ignored.

So here is a better idea. A targeted or 'strings attached' tax credit for corporations and businesses. Do something good, get money back. *Cause and Effect. Equilibrium.* Eliminate Zog and his lazy, unmotivated tendencies. So how about a corporate tax credit for investing in a supplemental energy source like rooftop photovoltaic cells for your factory? A credit for the installation of charging stations for employees who drive electric or hybrid vehicles to work? Or a tax credit for successfully implementing the ISO14000 Environmental standard at the company. A tax credit for hiring and keeping a worker domestically? The list of targeted tax incentives for business is long. Of course, there is no arguing that this is a form of a subsidy. But not all subsidies are bad, especially if they modify economic behavior that is beneficial to the business over the long run, the Natural and Social Environments the business operates in and benefits the Common Good.

BREAKTHROUGH MOMENT

Some readers may have already extrapolated the Zog principle from how it works in the Economy to Education, where it applies equally as well. In order to avoid Zog, we routinely teach first and then test our children and assess our teachers on the acquisition and transfer of knowledge. We hand out a grade *depending* on the results of the test. Suppose instead we went Zog and said to our children; since you are all bright and above average and we like you, everyone gets an 'A' right now. We are going to assume that you successfully acquired the knowledge for the lesson and that the teacher was successful in delivering that service. Then we will have everyone take the test and further assume everyone did well. Of course we don't do this and would never think of assessing our students or teachers in this way! We want accountability. We want results linked to performance in our Education system.

So why in the world would anyone consider giving a no strings attached tax cut to any corporation? Are they somehow more worthy of our trust than our children or working professional adults? Forget it! Tax cuts to spur business hiring or investment must come with conditions. Strings definitely attached. Unless of course, you are an elected official with a very big corporation or lobbying group funding you.

ANOTHER BREAKTHROUGH MOMENT

It not really hard to see that the basic laws of Thermodynamics that govern systems and processes in our Natural Environment can also be easily applied to and describe economic systems and processes. After all the Economy is a *derived* system attached to the Environment. That is, economic systems cannot exist alone; they depend on the Environment and Energy to exist and run. Energy is also a derived system based on natural resource exploitation. It cannot stand alone; there has to be an Environment to provide resources to exploit first. Which lastly brings us to Education. The top derived system is the Education system because it ultimately depends on the other three systems, Environment, Energy and Economy. Imagine if we had no Environment, Energy or Economy; we would be teaching our children about nothing. That is supposing they could even exist in a world without a healthy Environment, without Energy and no Economy.

This revelation should also answer once and for all the question of why we start our critical thinking process with the Environment regardless of the situation. People in the Quality profession call this looking for the root cause; they always want to find out why something has failed or worn out prematurely. Good business people are always looking to define the parameters of a problem first before they gather data, measure it, analyze the results and implement a plan of action. In each case there are Environmental variables or constants at the core that will guide their thinking.

Some folks think of the Environment unconsciously when presented with a problem; gee…how is that increase in my oil bill going to affect my Family Environment? What if I don't pay it on time and it is a cold winter and the heat goes out? But many, many more skip it entirely; especially elected officials and politicians who need to ignore inconvenient facts in order to support preconceived notions or positions that may have special benefits for the few and have no benefit the Common Good.

E EDUCATION
N
V
I
R   *"Without an education you aren't*
O ECONOMY   *going anywhere in this world."*
N   Guess who said that? Malcolm X.
M   He never finished his formal
E   schooling beyond age fifteen and
N   completed his studies organi-
T E N E R G Y cally while contemplating his life
behind bars in a Massachusetts prison for committing
petty crimes. He was self schooled. Malcolm X had his
radical origins but went on to become a ground break-
ing civil rights leader in his era. Despite his lack of formal
higher education, Malcolm X instinctively knew what a
good education meant to all the people in this world. In
his later years Malcolm X became a forceful advocate for
Education and saw the tremendous opportunities a proper
Education imparted including social justice and economic
advancement, particularly for African American children.
He knew a good Education would allow people of all races
to successfully manage the levers and resources of all the
Environments we inhabit.

Malcolm X knew Education was not an exclusive
realm. In any successful crusade for human rights and the
Common Good everyone needs to be aware of the human
condition and have ideas on how to improve it. "X' has

meant and does mean many different things to different people. I believe 'X' means Education for all of us. In order to have a successful nation and a just and fair society going forward everyone must have the benefits of a good Education.

So where does Education stand in our hierarchy of thinking? It is the top most horizontal beam of our letter 'E' presiding over the Economy and Energy and attached to the Environment. It relies heavily on principle number two; individual self worth and the promotion of this human quality for maximum benefit to the individual and hopefully, to society as a whole.

It is not the intention here to advocate any particular teaching pedagogy currently used in Education over something else, but rather focus on basic and obvious learning methods that have lately been subverted for one reason or another. The attempt here is to find some good ideas and incorporate them into a larger cohesive and efficient system of Education that puts our children's learning needs first. It does not matter whether the learning is occurring at a public school, a charter school or a private one; the basic ideas and tools to teach are not the unique property of any particular Education system or environment.

So let us begin our discussion of Education with Environment. As we have seen in the Natural Environment, the 'unlimited growth' or 'unlimited resource' models of projecting the future performance of a human activity is fundamentally flawed. Yet most all of the reform movements in Education are based on some 'unlimited growth' model; merit pay for teachers based on the teacher's ability to generate year over year gains in student performance based on arbitrary objective student testing. Think about this for a moment and any one with common sense and the ability to break down this Education reform model into manageable parts will see the entire model to be unsustainable and absurd.

It is easy; first take out all the variability in the student body and assume that all students are from the same socio-economic background. Let us next assume the student exams have no bias and that the questions test the same knowledge in the same format year after year.

At some point, two solid walls are hit; the first being the human mind. There is only so much that a 12 year old mind (or any mind for that matter) can absorb. Biology is a limitation. Secondly, the teacher and the reform model run right smack into good old fashioned bell curve statistics. The student exam results will cluster over a period of time; most children will perform around the statistical mean in the center of the bell curve, a small percentage will perform better and a small percentage worse. Always and forever. So what are we supposed to do with the teacher's pay? Freeze it? The teacher has no control over biology or the statistical tendencies found in nature and society. The teacher still has a mortgage to pay, food to buy and has to put gas in her car to get to school. There is Economic inflation from human activity. Is the teacher supposed to slowly go broke teaching? Or start broke in an overcrowded classroom? Everyone with common sense we see this is a ridiculous conclusion but it is the logical one given the ridiculous premise of ever increasing student performance.

DIFFERENT APPROACHES TO SCHOOLS

Over the years various proposals for the proper schooling of our children have put many different types of schools out there as alternatives to traditional public schools; charter schools, magnet schools, Montessori schools, parochial school, the list goes on. Not one of these alternatives has been able to show better long lasting results over the public schools.

There are mountains of data showing that students at charter schools are no better performing and sometimes perform worse than students at the public schools. A landmark 2009 study by a pro charter school group funded by the Walton family and the Michael and Susan Dell Foundation bears this out; it should not be a surprise.

And what of evil teacher's unions? If teacher's unions are so evil why are the worst performing public schools in right to work states in the South and West? Why are some of the best performing public schools in the nation located in suburban New York and New Jersey? School Districts solidly in the grips of powerful teachers unions? Again, this is pernicious scapegoating that flies in the face of commons sense.

Public Schools are still the best choice for the vast majority of today's students. In fact, a conservative argument can be made that our nation's public schools are worth saving precisely because they are the nation's traditional schools with roots going back to Horace Mann. And as the traditional method of education, public schooling must be preserved, modified and supported as the best education alternative for our children. There are ways to supplement this aging Education system without throwing it out completely or radically overhauling it. A particular example to highlight is the State of Maine independent school system. This education system works in a complimentary fashion with the state public education system.

In the state of Maine, there exists a public system of education and a quasi-public system known as town tuitioning. This system grew out of necessity in a sparsely populated, mostly rural state. Many towns either could not afford or did not want to build their own high schools. In 1909 the State of Maine passed legislation requiring the towns to either build a high school or send their children to another school. The students' tuition to the selected school is picked up by all the town residents with the rate set by the state. Families have the choice where to send their children for an Education, either another public school or an independent school. There are currently ten independent schools in the State. This is not a charter school system. Maine does not have a charter school law.

What this 1909 law has done is allow students from poor rural or urban backgrounds to attend a high school of choice, often an independent boarding school located in the State. An in-state town tuition student does not have to take entrance exams, but the behavior, character and academic standing of the student is monitored by the independent school authority. Tuition for the independent school is paid for by public tax dollars. These independent schools have small class sizes, adhere to state Education standards and attract other students from around the world creating a small, diverse classroom learning environment. A child from Aroostook County may be sitting next to a child from China. This is precisely the Social Environment that is best to foster learning; small class size, intimate contact between students and teachers, students and students and diversity. It is the type of learning environment in which teaching tools such as scaffolding or inquiry based instruction can really be exercised to maximum benefit. While this quasi-public system of Education may not work in every state, it is worth taking a look at to see if there are opportunities to emulate the model in other Social Environments.

CURIOSITY: FROM THE CONCRETE TO THE ABSTRACT

Children are naturally curious; they need to feel they are connected to the world in order to learn better. The connection should be real, not abstract or disconnected. Young children especially are not abstract or critical thinkers. Children advance their learning from the concrete to the abstract as their brains develop from infancy all the way into their twenties, so why do many early lessons in school stand apart from the Natural and Social Environments? They should not. One and one make two. To a child, so what? This is too abstract for their brains to comprehend. Connect this simple exercise in addition to something that is real and concrete to them; not dots or images on a computer screen. One finger plus one finger makes two fingers on your hand. One wheel plus another wheel on a bicycle make two wheels. Talk about the wheel; what shape is it? How does it turn? Anything that children in a particular Community Environment experience everyday can work to make learning and the acquisition of knowledge real and tangible. Scale this thinking up to accommodate more mature minds. Always move from the concrete to the abstract when teaching a new subject. Lessons should have a context to them that stresses the connection a child has to their peers in the classroom, the immediate Natural Environment and to the Family and Community Environment in which they function everyday. This is the best way to tap into a child's natural curiosity.

SCAFFOLDING: A NEGLECTED TOOL OF THE TRADE

The oldest teaching tool available to humans is something called Scaffolding and it works in the context of the Social Environment. The concept is so easy and makes so much common sense that it is frightening.

Scaffolding as a teaching strategy originates from Lev Vygotsky's sociocultural theory and his concept of the *zone of proximal development* (ZPD). "The zone of proximal development is the distance between what children can do by themselves and the next learning that they can be helped to achieve with competent assistance."

In scaffolding instruction a more knowledgeable other provides scaffolds or supports to facilitate the learner's development. Scaffolding can be visualized as a ladder with steps that are used to develop the student's ability to build on prior knowledge and internalize new information. The activities provided in scaffolding instruction are just beyond the level of what the learner can do alone. The more capable other provides the scaffolds so that the learner can accomplish (with assistance) the tasks that he or she could otherwise not complete, thus helping the learner through the zone of proximal development.

An important aspect of scaffolding instruction is that the scaffolds are temporary. As the learner's abilities increase the scaffolding provided by the more knowledgeable other is progressively withdrawn. Finally the learner is able to complete the task or master the concepts independently. Therefore the goal of the educator when using the scaffolding teaching strategy is for the student to become an independent and self-regulating learner and problem solver.

In order to get the best learning results with scaffolding, children need personal, trustworthy and intimate contact with a skilled instructor. A teacher trying to manage an overcrowded class of thirty children cannot use the scaffolding tool to any good effect on a consistent basis.

In addition to teachers, caregivers and parents help young children learn how to link old information or familiar situations with new knowledge through verbal and nonverbal communication and modeling behaviors. Observational research on early childhood learning shows that parents and other caregivers facilitate learning by providing scaffolds. The scaffolds provided are activities and tasks that:

- Motivate or enlist the child's interest related to the task
- Simplify the task to make it more manageable and achievable for a child

- Provide some direction in order to help the child focus on achieving the goal
- Clearly indicate differences between the child's work and the standard or desired solution
- Reduce frustration and risk
- Model and clearly define the expectations of the activity to be performed.

The outcomes from using scaffolding as a teaching approach are summarized as:

- Pointing students to worthy sources – educators provide sources to reduce confusion, frustration, and time. The students may then decide which of these sources to use.
- Reduces uncertainty, surprise, and disappointment – on the part of the students and the Educators.

Following the use of teacher provided scaffolds, the educator may then have the students engage in cooperative learning. In this type of environment students help other students in small group settings but still have some teacher assistance. This can serve as a step in the process of decreasing the scaffolds provided by the educator and needed by students

Scaffolding is also easier to implement if there are more qualified instructors present in the learning environment or less students or a combination of both. A single teacher and maybe an aide trying to control a class of thirty or forty students in a forty minute time period does not leave much time for close, meaningful teacher and student interaction. Class sizes must be smaller. It is interesting to note that one room school houses with a single teacher, no administrators and a mix of children from all socio-economic backgrounds and ages actually may be a good model for what has to happen in Education today. Think about the immediate enriching small Community Environment these children were immersed in. Think about the teacher and older skilled children that the younger children had access to in order to learn their lessons. Many great people learned and learned well in this old time Education environment. While the one room school may be hopelessly outdates in some respects, it should not be dismissed and can be a jumping off point when thinking about how to improve Education.

Despite the obvious positive qualities of scaffolding as a teaching tool, it is being subverted and neglected in all Education environments. Many believe that technology can do it better. But technology is the tool, not the teacher. A hammer cannot by itself show someone how to put a roof on a house. Technology has no personality on its own and no stake in the child's Education.

CONNECTING EDUCATION
TO OUR ENVIRONMENT

Our public education system has become detached from our Social and Natural Environments. The greatest, most useful and proven tool of instruction, scaffolding has been taken away from our teachers by class sizes that are too large and bureaucracies that want our teachers to do everything else but teach. The modern teacher must be a social worker, a substitute parent, and a manager who is available and accountable every day all day to students, parents, administrators and politicians. Parents are excused and absolved of all responsibility for the education of their children. This state of affairs undermines the primary mission of a teacher and that is to teach children and facilitate the acquisition of knowledge and skills necessary for success in this world. Teaching is not first anymore and it should be.

Many of our children are transported far away from home, put in an impersonal building walled off from nature and the surrounding community and experience learning as an antiseptic and detached exercise. Children are naturally curious but that curiosity is being dampened through mandatory testing, mountains of irrelevant homework and unnecessary indoctrination to the political wills of adults both near and distant who think they know better. Some folks have tried to address this lack of Family or Community Environment connection by home schooling. Religious schools try to instruct students with a common faith background. Both approaches have it partly correct but home schooling and faith oriented schools can be isolating and exclusionary. These approaches do not address the educational common good as envisioned by Horace Mann, the father of modern public school education in America.

We can enrich and fulfill our children's education needs and not have to do it by dividing them up according to faith or socioeconomic class. A classroom should not be homogenous environment but rather a diverse group of individuals who bring different experiences and points of view to the learning environment, thus enriching that environment. Learning has to be reattached to the diverse Natural and Social Environments in which children function in and will live in everyday for the rest of their lives. A reexamination of the relationship between the Environment and Education is necessary; only then can children begin to ask the relevant questions that will lead to learning, acquiring knowledge and becoming informed, critically thinking adults.

INQUIRY BASED EDUCATION

Hands on learning or inquiry based Education tap into a child's natural curiosity about the world around them and stress the child's role in the Natural Environment and their relationship to the Family and Community Environments they inhabit everyday.

Inquiry based learning is hands on; it requires students to approach a problem by asking questions, interacting with peers and formulating answers based on experiments, open communication, failure and feedback. Scaffolding is a major teaching tool that is used in inquiry based instruction.

Some school systems have taken this approach with particular attention to teaching science but there is no reason it cannot be implemented on a wider scale across other subjects. There are some obstacles to this. Inquiry based learning takes interaction between teacher and student and between student and student and can require more time more than the typical class period. And that period is often filled with the routines of attendance, homework review and testing requirements. Mandated material for the subject being studied must be covered over a set period of time. Despite these obstacles some creative teachers have found a way to implement inquiry based learning on a small scale in their classrooms. But bigger class sizes again limit the success of inquiry based instruction.

TEACHERS NEED TO TEACH

Another issue that gets in the way of good teaching is the expanding role of the teacher as mandated over the years by others outside the classroom. Teachers are asked to be social workers and psychoanalysts on top of being top notch instructors. They have been asked to be managers and negotiators. Mandated material and testing schedules chip away at valuable classroom time. Actual teaching time is being edged out by other responsibilities and requirements; some mundane, some well meaning and others of questionable value.

While some blame can be tossed squarely into the laps of remote bureaucrats, much of the blame must rest squarely with parents who have put those bureaucrats and officials in positions of power on their behalf to direct their children's Education. Education begins at home, in the Family Environment, with the molding of behavior and character. Parents need to be held responsible for their children's behavior, at home, at school and everywhere in between. Their responsibility does not end at the bus stop in the morning and pick up again after work. While teachers must be trained in spotting trouble signs with their students their responsibility must stop at reporting the behavior.

Assigned homework must be monitored at home. Assistance must be rendered by parents on assignments or that assistance found if it beyond the scope of the parents' abilities. Conversations must be had everyday at the dinner table between parents and their children about what they are learning. An engaged parent is the best educational partner a child can have. The love of learning starts at home and accountability rests with parents.

Given all that is at stake, Education does not need to onerous and heavy. Our children must love learning, be in good learning Environments and have the best teachers to instruct them. Allow teachers to actually teach. Smaller class sizes, the use of scaffolding and inquiry based Education tools and perhaps some form of school choice that does not dismantle the public system can improve the results of traditional public school Education in our nation.

Social Issues are what I term 'distracters' that are used by both current political parties and the news media in all its current forms to divert attention from or distract regular Americans away from the four core issues of Environment, Economy, Energy and Education.

It is quite easy to conjure up and invoke social issues that pull strongly on the emotions of any human. The new media and hard core, ideologically driven politicians can easily summon up statistically outlying examples of problems with abortion, the death penalty or drugs in order conjure up ratings or political points with the faithful. Extreme examples abound; the heinous rape and murder of a young girl in her own home, a mother in the second trimester of a pregnancy who will surely die if she carries the fetus full term, a brain dead person on life support with no clear intentions as to her future state of being after a terrible accident, forcing the family to make a life or death decision on her behalf.

These are easy issues to bring up when politicians have no easy answers to real problems, or do not want to tell the truth about the Environment, the Economy, Energy or Education. They are also good on a slow news day in the 24 hours news cycle. Why? Because terrible images wrapped around social issues tug at the non-rational, emotional heart strings of millions of Americans, evoking rage and

fear and non-pragmatic responses to events that unfortunately can and will happen in a country that is as diverse
and populous as ours. While it is right to feel outrage and
event righteous indignation at these terrible crimes and
events it is counter productive to enlist or shut down the
rational resources of this country, the President, the con-
gress and the courts. It is a bit like worrying about whether
Iran will develop a nuclear weapon or wringing your hands
over the first time your teenage daughter may have sex;
both events can and will happen.

With that said; it is not that we cannot do something
about abortion, the death penalty and drugs. But the fed-
eral government is a secular institution not suited to making broad generalized law based on the exceptionalism of a
few terrible cases of social malfeasance.

Questions and guidance on these social issues have
been effectively ceded over the years by families, churches,
synagogues and mosques to politicians and elected officials
who are not in a position to legislate on these deeply personal, moral and divisive issues. Indeed this is no way to
make law for the majority or the Common Good given the
diversity of religions, faiths, socioeconomic conditions and
the capacity for human folly in our nation and around the
world.

Seen through the lens of Environment and Education,
abortion is an issue best discussed in the Family Environment
in consultation with one's priest, rabbi, or imam with a
minimum of secular guidance from a state government.
Health comes to mind as the guiding secular, social issue.
Education of young men and women by their families

and through the churches, synagogues and mosques they belong to is the best approach to dealing with this issue outside the secular sphere, keeping in mind that under the best of circumstances, with the most well spun social contract at the Family and Community Environment levels some abortions will still occur.

But this does not mean our critical thinking processes cannot be applied to some aspects of the broader social issues. For the sake of brief illustration, let us take a focused look at abortion and the death penalty and see what happens.

Abortion always manages to be a hot issue in the realm of public discourse. Unfortunately it occurs all too often for the wrong reasons and given the enormous human population and diversity of conditions is probably something that should never have to occur but will still happen. Given this backdrop, the procedure does represent a health issue in the Social Environment and a failing in the Education of our young people. Volumes have been written on this issue as a whole from both sides and it is not the intention to repeat any of the arguments here, so let us look at some smaller aspect of the issue.

Consider the public funding of the abortion procedure by the state. As a health issue, a small part of one half the population of our nation considers and follows through with an abortion, sometimes at public expense. Is it in the interest of the Common Good to subsidize this procedure? Should the greater communities that the individual inhabits foot the bill? If we do this for abortion services than why not heart disease or prostate cancer?

Both health issues affect a portion of the population and left unchecked, both heart disease and prostate cancer will eventually cause death. This is certain. So why not publicly fund these health issues? It does not take long to see that any argument for the public funding of abortion breaks down in the face of rational and reasonable analysis.

Now look at the death penalty. A heinous crime against a family or an entire community occurs. Is it in the interest of the Common Good to put the perpetrator to death? To use the social resources of our communities to capture, try, convict, appeal, detain and appeal again the perpetrator? Is death the easy out for the criminal? How about thinking about it for the rest of their lives without chance of parole in a very small, locked room? The impact of this human decision on all Environments will be felt for a very long time.

What are we really punishing with the application of the death penalty? There clearly has been a failure of the Social Environment at many levels for the perpetrator and on the part of the unfortunate victim. Safety from harm was not ensured. Were economic forces to blame? The lack of opportunity? Was there a failure in Education that contributed to the violent act? Was the perpetrator just plain crazy, an outlier produced by nature or was this just a random act of violence? Capital punishment in any case can not be undone if we are wrong about the circumstances and judgment of the crime.

What does it mean when the facts on the ground state that over one hundred people would have been wrongfully executed in this nation due to irrational or poor application of the social laws and tools used to capture, try by jury and administer punishment for crimes involving the death of another human being? Criminal and judicial system failures and fear may kill innocent people and probably have since the time of the Salem witch trials early in the history of this nation. Cause and Effect breaks down in the face of fear. Irrationality rules the day on all levels of the Social Environment. Given this quick review, it would be prudent to stay rational, face fear, be bigger than the criminals and seek a punishment, no matter how hateful or heinous the act, without the finality and social ambivalence of the death penalty. If states insist on keeping this punishment on the books one can at least make the argument not to enforce it.

....

While social issues can be addressed using our principles and through our framework of critical thinking it is best to break the issue up into manageable components and then analyze each component separately to arrive at appropriate solutions. Sometimes a few of the components of the social issue need modification to achieve a measure of satisfaction, in other instances it is the whole of the issue that needs addressing. One can also have cases when, taken together the solutions tendered on various components may not add up to a cohesive or consistent whole solution for the social issue. It is also valuable to recognize a social issue as a distracting one as quickly as possible and then understand the possible exploitative motivations behind it before moving forward. Sometimes a distracter is best left alone.

Hopefully astute readers will come to realize that one of the underlying and unstated goals of this critical thinking exercise has been to strive to make ourselves a better society. Less division, less violence, less war, economic opportunity and better education for everybody, more of the golden rule and sensible use of all the faculties and resources at our command are essential to create a rational and just society.

6: CONCLUSIONS

Environment. Energy. Economy. Education. This is the framework for critical, objective reasoning when faced with issues and problems. This book was not really about what to think but rather how to think critically.

One of the lessons drawn is that best solutions, those that are arrived at objectively and pragmatically and those that consider all the available facts do not fit into current political paradigms. Best solutions are not meant to please everyone emotionally or politically, but they are the best solutions. What is implied throughout the analysis is that solutions need implementation and also control. What this means is that a solution to an issue or problem may be correct given the present set of facts but should be allowed to evolve if facts change. The Environment, Energy, Economy and Education framework for critical thinking is then reapplied and the implementation of solutions is reconsidered and monitored.

Here is a recap of what we have discovered; Hydraulic Fracturing: not the best method for natural gas extraction. Natural gas for power generation is good and cannot be thrown out of the Energy mix, fracking does not generate the profits anticipated and fracking for natural gas in the greater Catskills Region of New York is not a good idea. It could however, make sense in other communities.

Nuclear Energy has a problem with waste storage that can be overcome. Nuclear power is necessary to keep in our Energy mix and probably should be expanded in order to meet the needs of a growing, more sophisticated human population.

An Unrestrained Corporate Tax cut is a bad idea but business tax cuts with enforceable requirements is a good idea. Accountability is preserved and the maximum positive benefits accrue to the most possible stakeholders in the fairest way possible.

The best Education our children can get will be in small, diverse classes with well paid teachers using natural teaching tools like scaffolding. The acquisition of knowledge on various subjects and tasks should be relevant and tie into all the communities children live in and interact with.

Another important point made throughout our exploration of critical thinking and ideas is the movement of thought from the concrete to the abstract. It is important to recognize this mode of learning as the dominant mode of knowledge acquisition in humans and then exercise it as we work towards solutions to the various problems facing us as a society. At this point, you should be an educated reader who can use the knowledge gained and apply it to the issues and problems of your choice.

Our nation is an exceptional one and can only continue to be so if the exploitation of a trusting electorate by an entrenched political power structure is stopped and the power to govern is given back to those who consent to be governed. The various liberties and freedoms we take for granted are not ensured and protected by physical weapons but by the weapon of the well informed mind that is; a citizenry able to think independently and rationally is the best guarantor of liberty and freedom not just in America but around the world.

7: AFTERWORD

Surely some of the conclusions drawn on hydraulic fracturing, nuclear power and tax cuts raised a few eyebrows. What many a reader may have noticed is that the conclusions do not necessarily fit neatly into current political alignments and nor were they supposed to. Best solutions can have a political component to them but more often than not the political component is not the major component. A best solution is designed to solve a problem in the most pragmatic, realistic way possible and make the most people happy; it is a solution that serves the Common Good, but this implies that some folks are not going to be happy. We as a nation need to get over this. Not everyone is going to be happy politically or emotionally with a best solution, but throughout our history, we as a nation have made tough choices and worked it out as a community with common goals. We do not seem to have the will to do this anymore.

Politics has presently become just another form of entertainment or politainment. Not that there never was an entertainment aspect to politics. But politicians and elected officials have too recently been foolish with the responsibilities we have entrusted to them and it is my hope that more than a few will read this book and implement the Environment, Energy, Economy and Education critical thinking framework with respect to the four core principles of Cause and Effect, Self Worth, the Common Good and Interrelation.

Another point worth making is the lack of any references or footnotes. I made the decision early on not to reference or source anything in this book. Every idea or fact presented in these pages is easily referenced by opening a high school or college textbook or through a few clicks on the internet. All the ideas have been with us since the dawn of civilization; long before Lev Vygotsky was born (and has since died) scaffolding has been a teaching tool. The laws of Thermodynamics have been well known since man first discovered how to make fire; it has only been in the last few hundred years scientists have gotten around to writing them down. So in the end, I have not presented anything new; just a framework for thinking based on established ideas, laws of nature and principles that I hope more people will adopt into their own thinking.